THE MODERN AFRICAN COMMUNITY

Africa's Path To Prosperity

By:

JZK & AJ

Table of
CONTENTS

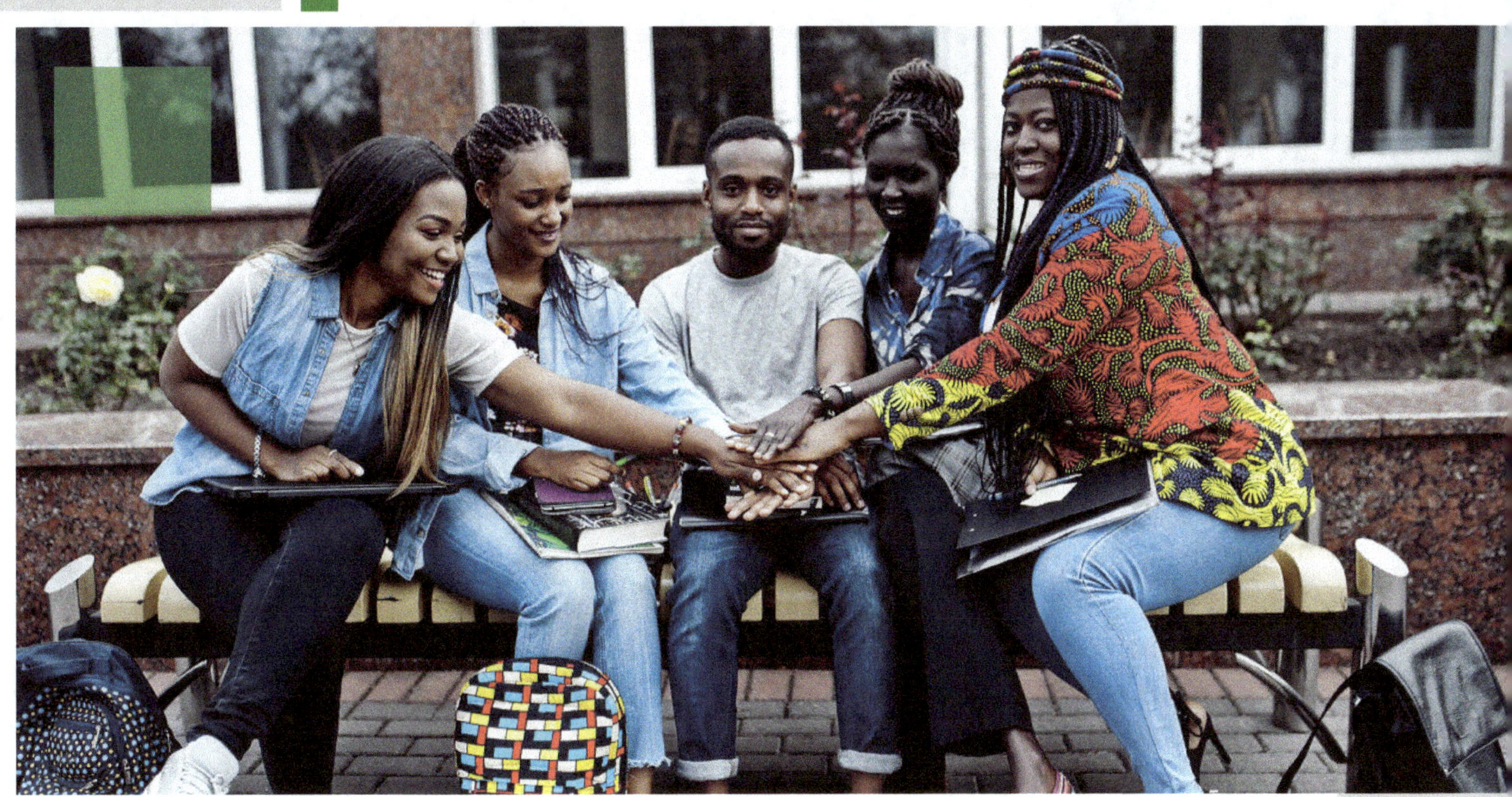

THE POWER OF COMMUNITY: THRIVING TOGETHER

Introduction

I wrote this book for everyone that has ever wondered why the Black/African community is lagging behind the rest of the world in terms of economic output, technology & development I have spent over 10 years of my life looking into what makes other communities thrive and what we could do as Africans to improve our lot on this planet. I dedicate this book to all the great African leaders that gave their blood, sweat and tears to try to advance our cause.

There are too many to name, but much love and respect to the likes of TBA, PBT, Irritated Genie, SWP, H.E Marcus Garvey, Dr. Khalid Muhammad, Cheikh Anta Diop, Chancellor Williams and the living legend, the good doctor, Dr. Claude Anderson. I don't have the words to express my gratitude for the wisdom and your valiant effort to advance your people, but I hope my dearest sentiments reach you.

Our Belief: Community is the Path to Success for Africans
We explore how being part of a community can help you advance in life, build powerful connections, and shape successful societies even in a hostile nation or enviroment.

GROUP ECONOMICS AND ITS IMPORTANCE

Group economics is absolutely vital for a community to thrive. It's the lifeforce and blood that allows a community to succeed and expand. Without it, you have no community, you just have a bunch of people living close to each other. People in a community come together, share their resources, talents, know-how and efforts to build collective wealth that benefits everyone in the community. The main idea in group economics is that getting ahead financially is not just one person's job but something everyone in the community can work on together. When people join forces with their money, communities can set up a solid foundation for stability and growth that empowers and enriches everyone.

One big part of group economics is about putting resources together. Come together as a group and establish things, like community banks, cooperative businesses and joint investment projects. When communities pool their money, they can get funds for starting businesses, building roads & parks, and other capital heavy projects like a real estate development that would be tough to carry out alone.

Group economics is about supporting the local businesses in the community. By choosing to buy local, community members keep money circulating within their own economy. This helps create a strong economic base, supporting job creation, building up skills, and keeping the wealth within the community. Supporting local businesses becomes a way to make the community financially independent and less reliant on outside economic forces. This is especially important for black people living in countries that are openly or implicitly against the advancement of African people.

Education and sharing knowledge are key to making group economics work well. Communities that talk about money, learn about it together, and share what they know empower everyone to make smart choices about their resources. This focus on education not only makes community members financially better off but also strengthens the overall economic picture, building a culture where everyone is informed and takes part in economic decisions.

Group economics becomes really important when we think about fixing big economic inequalities. Some communities may have a hard time accessing regular banks or financial help. With group economics, these communities can create their own banks, lending programs, or investment groups, making sure they have the capital to build the institutions & public goods & services that's needed in their community. But if we were to sum up group economics into a simple sentence to remember it would be; group economics is about buying, selling, hiring and offering opportunities to the community first and foremost.

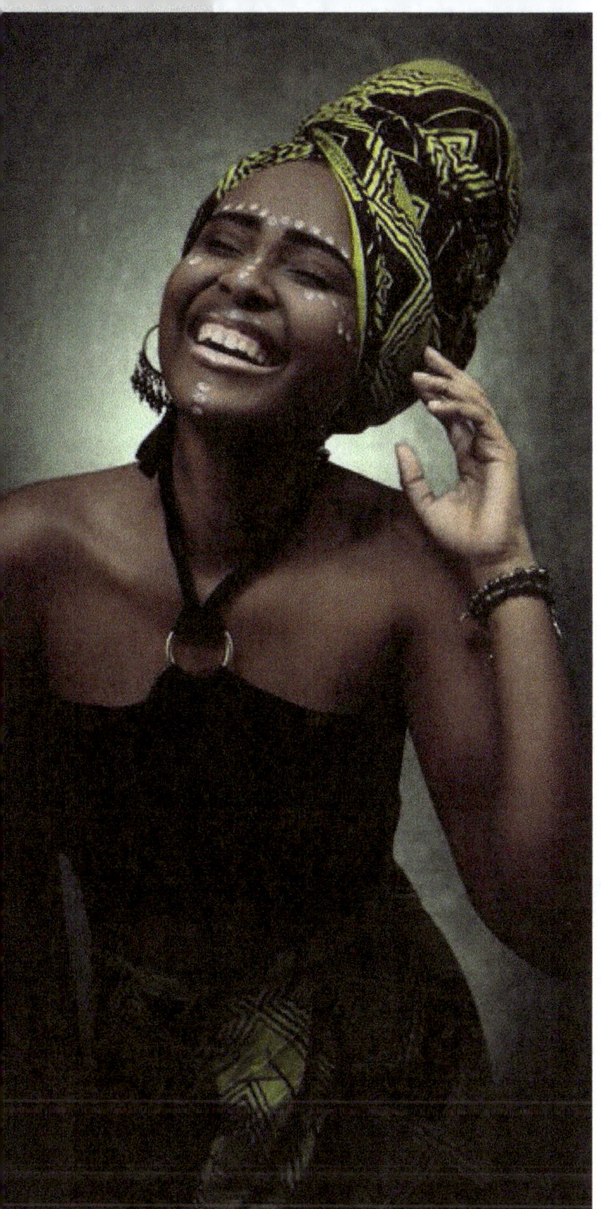

CHAPTER ONE

UNDERSTANDING COMMUNITY

What Is Community?

Community according to Wikipedia is a social unit or a group of living things with a shared socially significant characteristic, such as place, set of norms, culture, religion, values, customs, or identity. Communities may share a sense of place situated in a given geographical area (e.g. a country, village, town, or neighborhood) or in virtual space through communication platforms.

But we see community as a group of people that come together under a common value system (code of conduct) and practice group economics with each other in order for the group to benefit as a collective, usually within a specified geographical area where they control the politics (the laws/powers), the businesses (the economy) and the culture (the beliefs, traditions & behavior).

Common Value Systems

Different communities have different value systems, but some common value systems can be seen in most thriving communities. One big thing is treating each other with respect and kindness. In thriving communities, everyone values each person, making a place where differences are celebrated. This makes a pact for everyone to get along and work together.

Not just individuals, but the whole community also values teamwork. They care about everyone's well-being and working together. This team spirit shows in community projects and traditions that remind everyone how strong they are when united.

Working together also means giving back, like helping neighbors or joining community events. This helps keep the community strong and connected. It's like a circle of support, where everyone helps each other out.

Another important value is honesty and doing the right thing. Trust is super important, and being open and fair helps to keep the community together. Communities that value trust & honesty, develop a strong sense of what's right and guide each other to make good choices.Nature is also valued, with many communities caring for the environment. They have customs, traditions and rituals to show their connection to nature and a commitment to sustainable living. This helps protect the resources that keep the community going. You can't have a sea-side community that doesn't respect the sea, because they'll soon pollute and over-fish the sea and their community will die out.

Family is a big deal too. Many communities see families as the heart of their group. They respect older members, pass down traditions, and make sure the next generations are cared for. It's like building blocks – families build up the whole community. Our opinion is that a family consists of a married man & woman that have committed to living their lives together, only once they've committed to each other and are financially capable should they consider bringing children into this world. A community can NOT grow if it doesn't value family (married man + married woman + children).

Education is another value that pops up a lot. Learning new things is seen as powerful and helps the whole community grow. It's like a belief that knowledge can change not just one person, but the entire community for the better. Education is very important and allows a community to grow and expand, you can not have a community where education and knowledge is not valued - you'll end up having a bunch of addicts & criminals with no discipline giving in to their most basic base desires and wasting their free-time blaming the world for their situation.

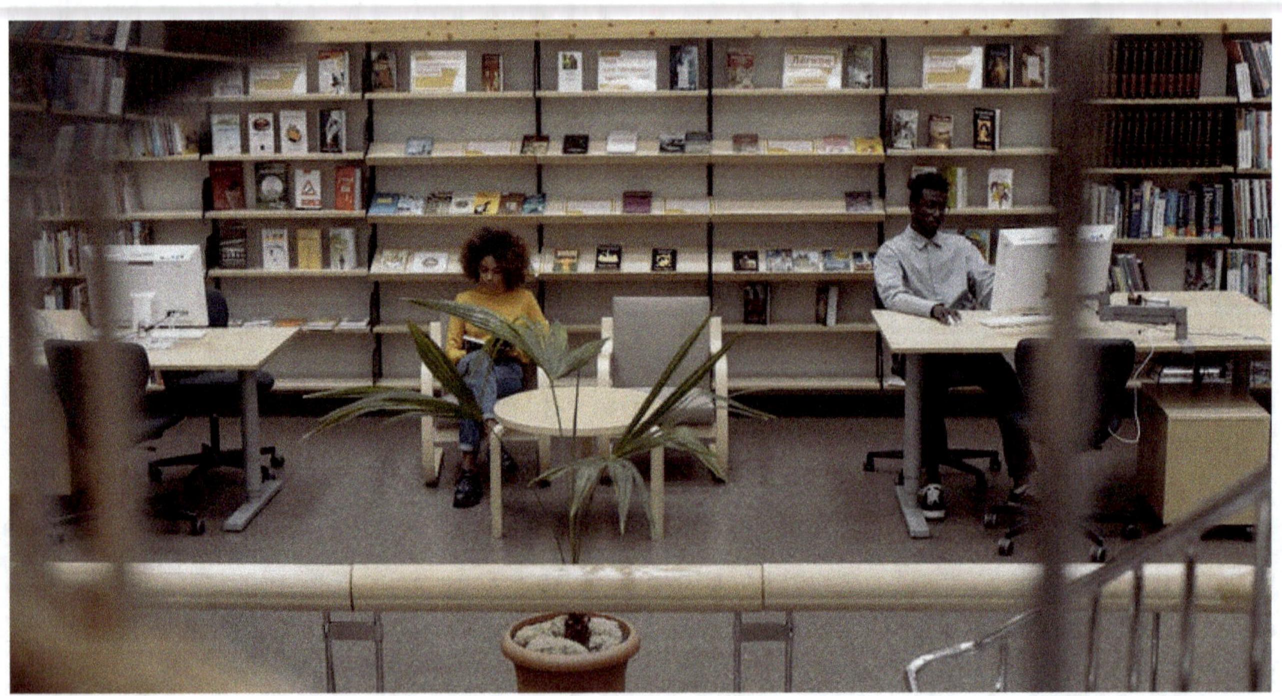

Varied Types Of Community

Communities play a pivotal role in shaping everyone, providing individuals with a sense of belonging, shared purpose, and mutual support. As diverse as humanity itself, communities come in various forms, each unique in its characteristics and dynamics.

Let's look at some of the types of communities that exist.

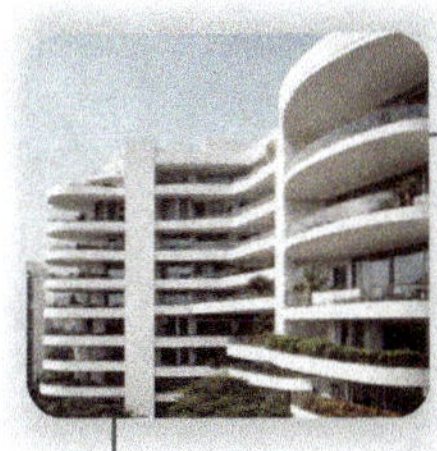

Geographic Communities:

Urban communities, bustling and diverse, thrive in cities where high population density fosters interactions and diversity. In contrast, rural communities, smaller in size, are known for their close-knit relationships and a more relaxed pace of life.

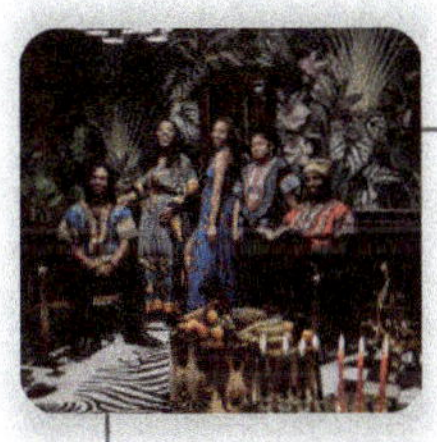

Cultural Communities:

Ethnic communities are bound by shared cultural heritage, language, traditions, and often a common ancestry. Religious communities, on the other hand, are formed around shared faith, beliefs, and religious practices, creating a deep sense of solidarity.

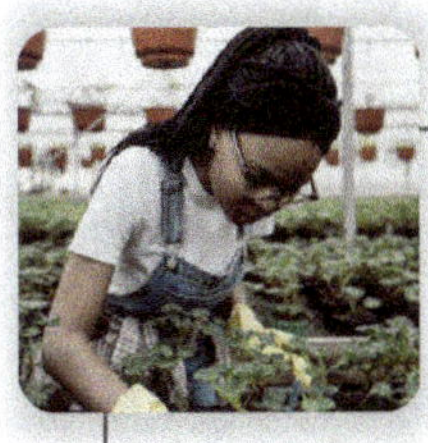

Interest-Based Communities:

These kinds of communities unite individuals with common interests or hobbies, whether it's gaming, gardening, or photography. Professional communities, rooted in common occupations or industries, provide platforms for networking and collaboration.

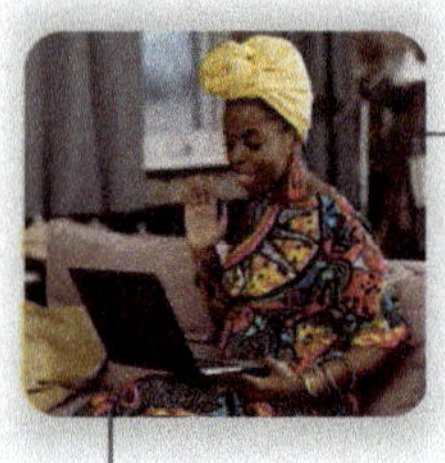

Virtual/Online Communities:

Social media platforms such as Facebook, Twitter, and Instagram connect people globally based on shared interests or relationships. Forums, meanwhile, serve as online spaces where individuals discuss specific topics, often under the veil of anonymity.

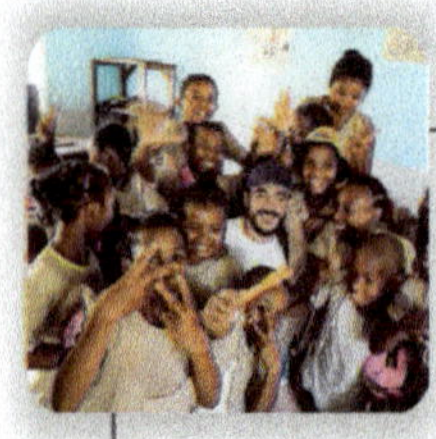

Educational Communities:

Academic communities form within educational institutions, including students, faculty, and staff. Online learning communities transcend physical boundaries, bringing together learners engaged in virtual courses or programs.

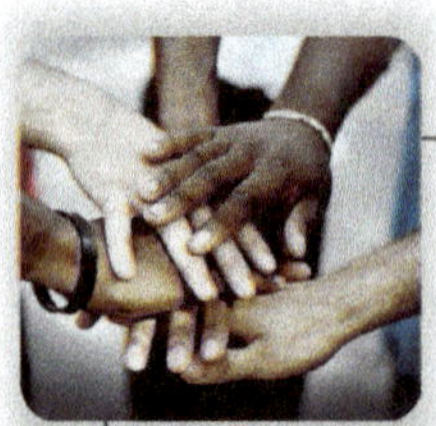

Support Communities:

Health communities offer support to individuals facing similar health challenges or conditions. Emotional support communities provide a space for individuals dealing with mental health issues, grief, or shared experiences.

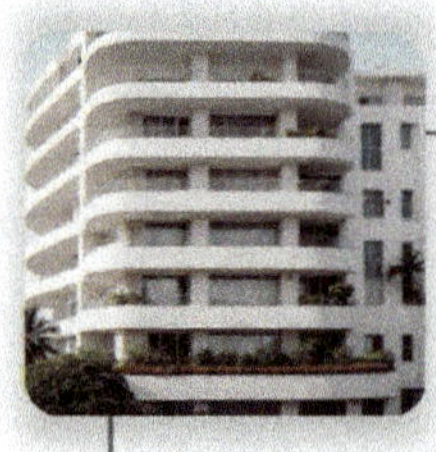

Membership-Based Communities:

Residential communities with restricted access, often focused on safety and shared amenities, define gated communities. Membership-based communities, such as exclusive clubs or societies, have specific entry criteria.

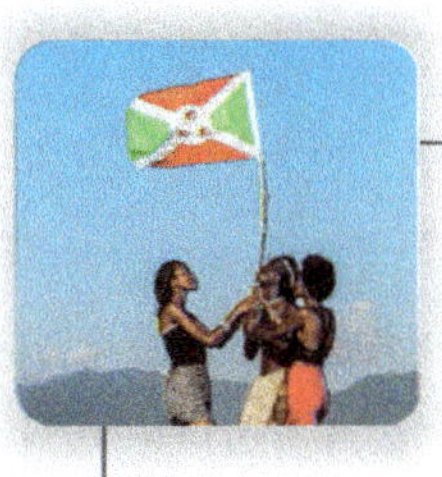

Environmental Communities:

Eco-friendly communities focus on sustainable living and environmental conservation. Outdoor enthusiasts find common ground in communities centered around activities like hiking, camping, bird watching or preserving the environment.

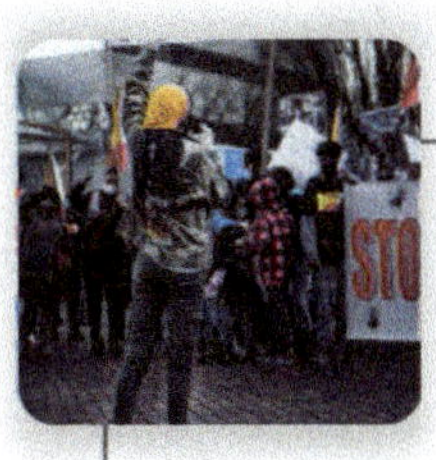

Political Communities:

Local political communities engage citizens in governance and community issues while advocacy groups, on the other hand, unite individuals supporting a particular cause or political ideology.

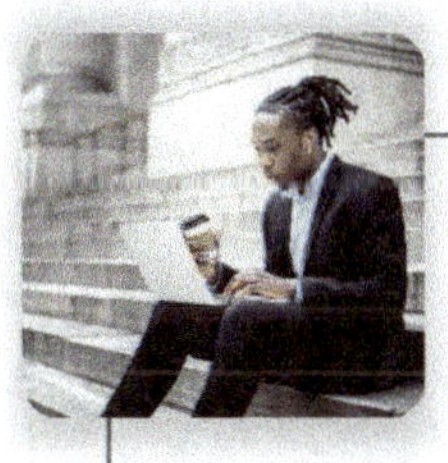

Economic Communities:

Business networks connect professionals within a specific industry or business sector. Cooperative communities emphasize shared ownership and decision-making, commonly seen in agriculture or business ventures.

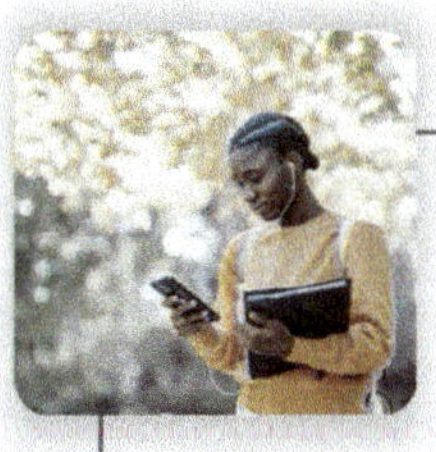

Generational Communities:

Youth groups bring together younger individuals for socializing and shared activities. Senior communities cater to the needs and interests of older adults, creating supportive environments for aging populations.

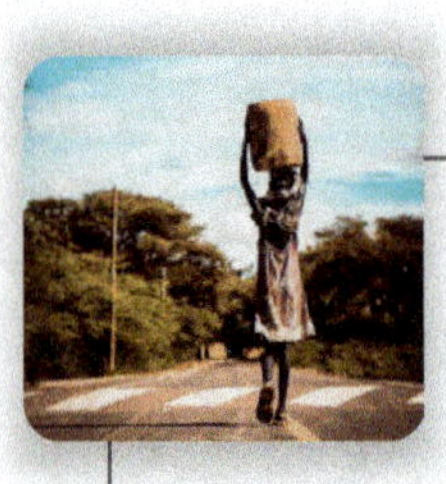

Volunteer Communities:

Service organizations engage individuals in charitable and community service activities, fostering a sense of purpose and giving back to society.

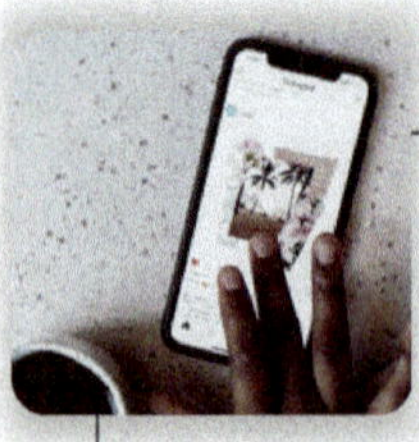

Civic Engagement Communities:

Activist groups focus on advocating for social or political change, while community development groups work towards improving local neighborhoods and infrastructure.

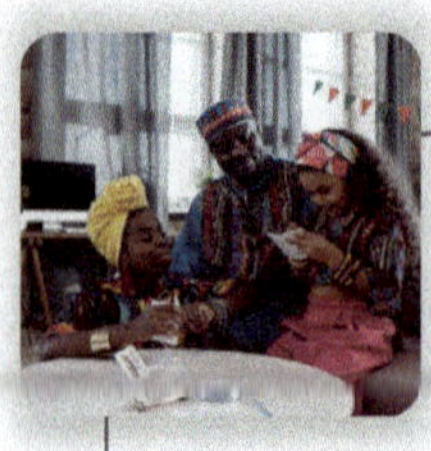

Family Communities:

Extended families, bound by blood ties, form large familial groups. In contrast, blended families comprise individuals from different family backgrounds, navigating the complexities of diverse relationships.

These are just some of the different types of communities that exist. Many people belong to more than just one community because different communities focus on delivering value in different areas. How many communities do you belong to right now? Why do you value those communities?

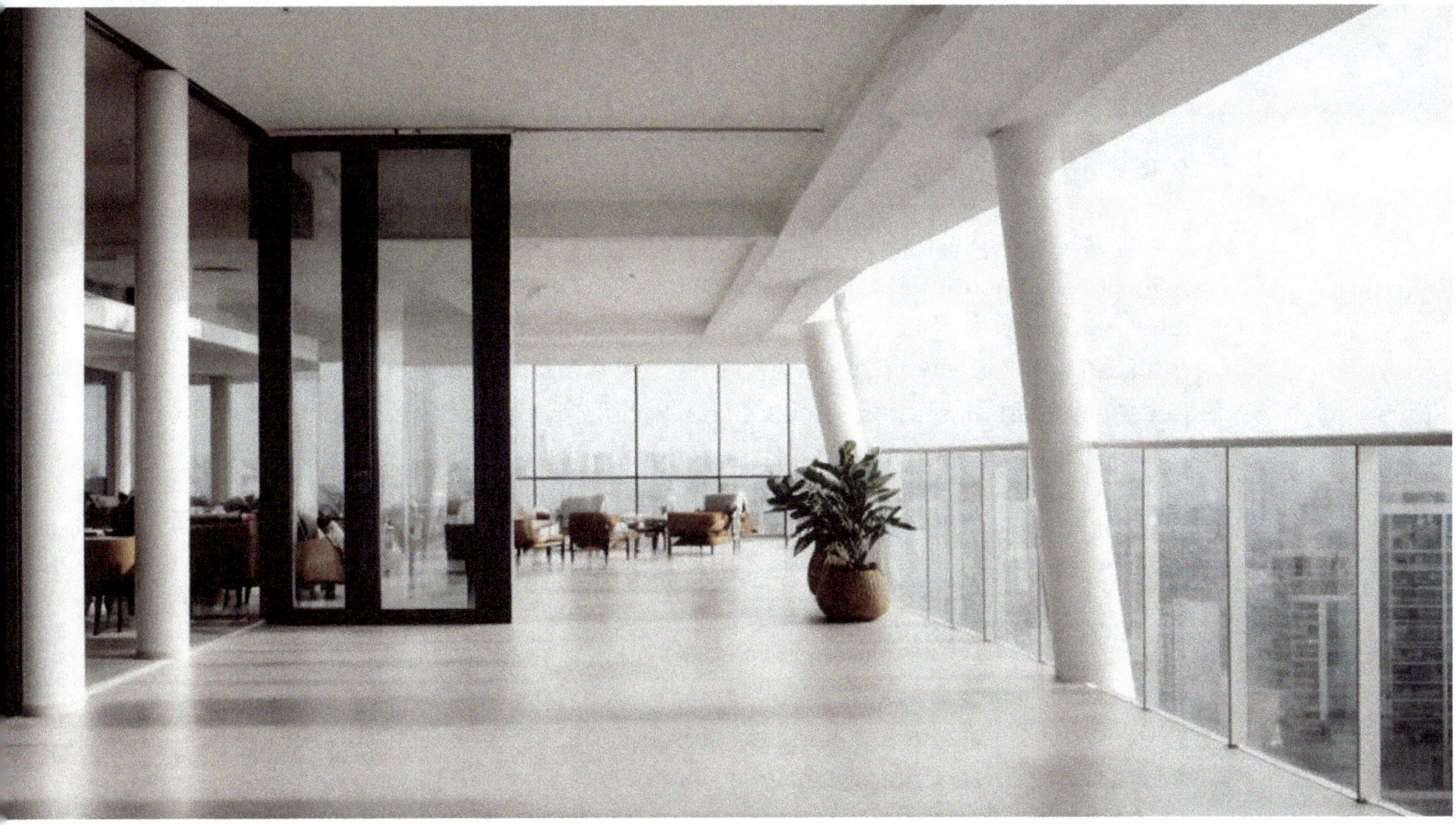

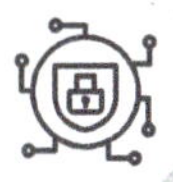

CHAPTER TWO

BENEFITS OF LIVING IN A COMMUNITY

Community/Group living, a fundamental aspect of human existence, offers a myriad of advantages that have shaped our evolutionary trajectory and continue to influence modern societies. From early human tribes to contemporary urban communities, the benefits of living in groups extend across various domains, encompassing survival, social interaction, and overall well-being.

01. Enhanced Security and Defense:

One of the primary benefits of community living lies in enhanced security and defense. Early humans found strength in numbers, providing protection against predators and other external threats. The collaborative efforts of a group allowed for shared vigilance, guarding against dangers that individuals alone would find challenging to overcome. This sense of collective security remains relevant today, as communities work together to address safety concerns.

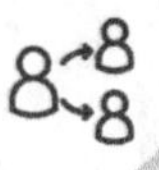

2. Resource Sharing and Cooperation:

Living in communities facilitates the sharing of resources and cooperative activities. Early human societies engaged in communal hunting, foraging, and later, agriculture. This cooperative approach maximized resource utilization, reduced individual workloads, and ensured a more efficient distribution of necessities. In modern contexts, this principle persists in shared economies, collaborative work environments, and communal resource management.

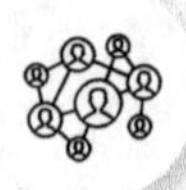

3. Social Support Networks:

Community living provides a built-in support system. Whether in times of crisis or everyday challenges, having a network of individuals with shared experiences fosters emotional well-being. The sense of belonging and mutual aid within a community contributes to the resilience of individuals, offering a buffer against stress and adversity. Social support networks play a crucial role in mental health and contribute to the overall quality of life.

4. Cultural Transmission and Learning:

Communities serve as a melting pot for cultural transmission and learning. Through interactions within groups, individuals absorb cultural values, traditions, and skills. This shared knowledge is passed down from generation to generation, contributing to the continuity of cultural practices. The collective wisdom within a community provides a rich environment for education and skill development.

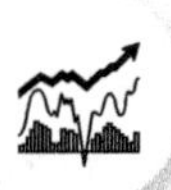

5. Economic Cooperation:

Group living facilitates economic cooperation, enabling the specialization of skills and the division of labor. In early human societies, this meant individuals could focus on specific tasks, such as hunting, farming, or crafting. In modern times, economic cooperation is evident in diverse industries, where collaboration and specialization contribute to economic growth and innovation.

6. Facilitation of Reproduction and Family Structures:

Community living is integral to the formation and sustainability of family structures. In early societies, the communal support system extended to childcare, ensuring the well-being and survival of offspring. This cooperative approach to reproduction persists in contemporary communities, where families benefit from the broader social fabric for support and assistance.

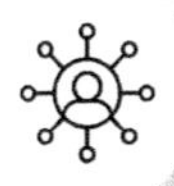

7. Social Bonding and Identity:

Living in a community fosters social bonding and the development of a shared identity. This sense of belonging contributes to a feeling of purpose and connection. Group identities can be based on factors such as culture, religion, or shared interests. This communal identity provides individuals with a sense of pride and affiliation, strengthening the social fabric.

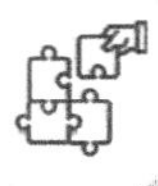

8. Efficient Problem-Solving and Decision-Making:

Communities provide a forum for collective problem-solving and decision-making. The diversity of perspectives within a group enhances the pool of ideas and approaches. This collaborative decision-making process often leads to more effective solutions, benefiting the entire community. Whether addressing challenges or planning for the future, group living allows for a comprehensive exploration of options.

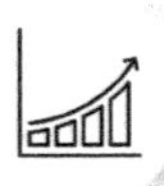

9. Increased Reproductive Success:

From an evolutionary standpoint, community living contributes to increased reproductive success. The protection, support, and resource-sharing within a community create favorable conditions for the survival and thriving of offspring. This reproductive advantage has played a pivotal role in the persistence of group living throughout human history.

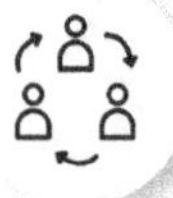

10. Social Interaction and Fulfillment:

Human beings are inherently social creatures, and group living fulfills the need for social interaction. Communities provide platforms for interpersonal relationships, fostering a sense of camaraderie and friendship. Social interactions contribute to emotional well-being, reducing feelings of isolation and loneliness.

Historical Perspective on Community Formation

People have always liked being together in groups throughout history. It's just a natural thing for humans to join up for help, safety, and working on things together. Looking back at history helps us understand how communities have changed and grown over time, and what made them come together in the first place.

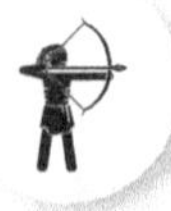

1. Early Hunter-Gatherer Bands:

The earliest human communities were nomadic bands of hunter-gatherers, forging a collective existence based on shared survival needs. These small, tightly-knit groups relied on collaboration for hunting, gathering, and shelter-building. The bonds formed within these bands were foundational to the development of communal living, laying the groundwork for the social structures that would evolve over millennia.

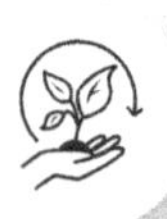

2. Transition to Agricultural Settlements:

The advent of agriculture marked a pivotal shift in community formation. As humans learned to cultivate crops and domesticate animals, settled agricultural communities emerged. Permanent settlements provided a stable foundation for larger populations, enabling the growth of more complex social structures. The transition to agriculture not only transformed the way communities sustained themselves but also laid the groundwork for cultural and economic specialization.

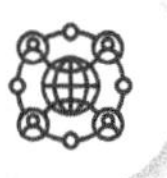

3. Ancient Civilizations:

Ancient civilizations, such as Mesopotamia, Egypt, the Indus Valley, and China, witnessed the formation of advanced urban communities. These civilizations marked the zenith of communal living with centralized governance, monumental architecture, and intricate social hierarchies. Cities became hubs of trade, culture, and administration, shaping the course of history through their contributions to art, science, and philosophy.

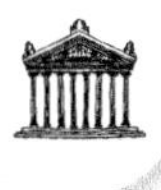

4. Greek City-States:

In ancient Greece, the city-state, or "polis," was a distinctive form of community. Greek city-states were characterized by a sense of civic pride, participatory governance, and a shared cultural identity. These communities played a pivotal role in the development of democracy, philosophy, and the arts, leaving an enduring legacy that influenced later concepts of civic engagement.

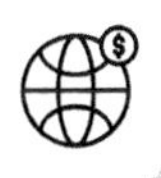

5. Medieval Towns and Guilds:

During the medieval period, the rise of towns and guilds marked a shift in community dynamics. Towns served as centers of commerce and culture, fostering the development of trade networks and specialized craftsmanship. Guilds, associations of skilled artisans, provided a framework for economic cooperation and mutual support, contributing to the economic and social fabric of medieval communities.

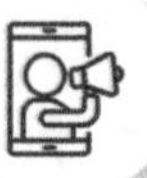

6. Renaissance and Urban Renaissance:

The Renaissance witnessed a revival of interest in classical ideals and humanism, influencing the structure of communities. Urban centers experienced a renaissance of their own, with flourishing arts, commerce, and intellectual pursuits. The emergence of a middle class played a crucial role in shaping the dynamics of these communities, as did the exchange of ideas facilitated by increased literacy and the printing press.

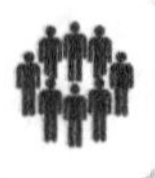

7. Enlightenment and the Birth of Modern Communities:

The Enlightenment era ushered in a new era of intellectual and social change, influencing the formation of modern communities. Enlightenment ideals, such as reason, liberty, and equality, contributed to the emergence of more inclusive and egalitarian communities. Concepts of citizenship and individual rights gained prominence, laying the groundwork for the evolution of democratic societies.

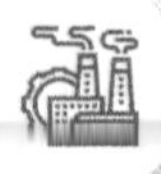

8. Industrial Revolution and Urbanization:

The Industrial Revolution brought about profound changes in community formation. The shift from agrarian economies to industrialized societies led to urbanization on an unprecedented scale. Industrial towns and cities became focal points of economic activity, with large populations drawn to factory work. This period saw the emergence of new social challenges and the formation of labor movements advocating for workers' rights.

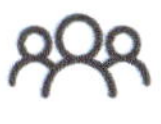

9. 20th Century Community Dynamics:

The 20th century witnessed diverse forms of community development. Suburbanization, driven by technological advancements and transportation improvements, led to the growth of residential communities outside urban centers. Social movements, such as civil rights and feminism, reshaped the dynamics of communities by advocating for inclusivity and equal rights. The global interconnectedness brought about by technology further transformed the concept of community, allowing for transnational connections and collaborations.

10. Contemporary Community Formation:

In the 21st century, community formation continues to evolve in response to technological, economic, and cultural shifts. Online communities, facilitated by the internet and social media, transcend geographic boundaries, allowing individuals to connect based on shared interests or identities. The concept of community has become more fluid, encompassing virtual spaces and diverse subcultures, challenging traditional notions of physical proximity as a prerequisite for communal bonds.

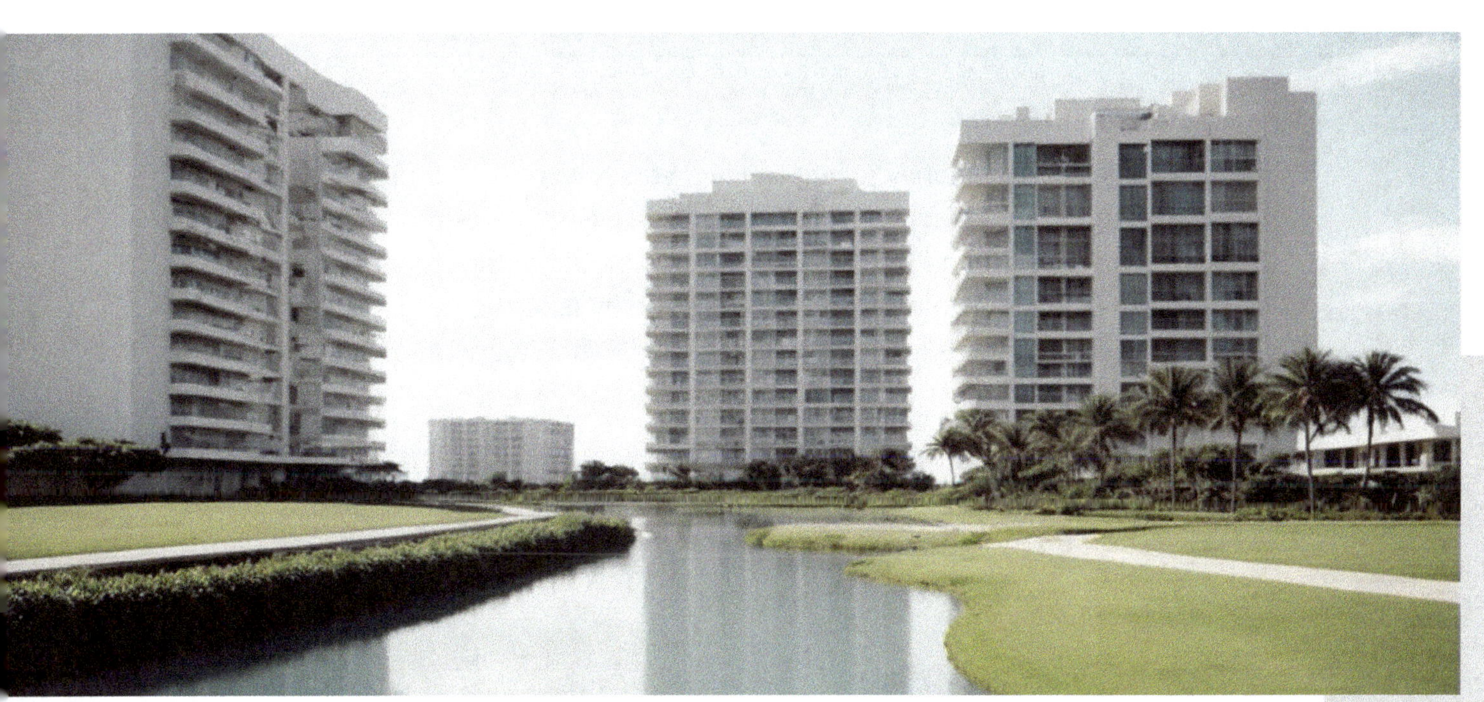

CHAPTER THREE

CASE STUDIES

Let's look at some of the notable communities and how they have evolved to this point.

We believe that we can learn from their success as we also seek to establish successful communities.

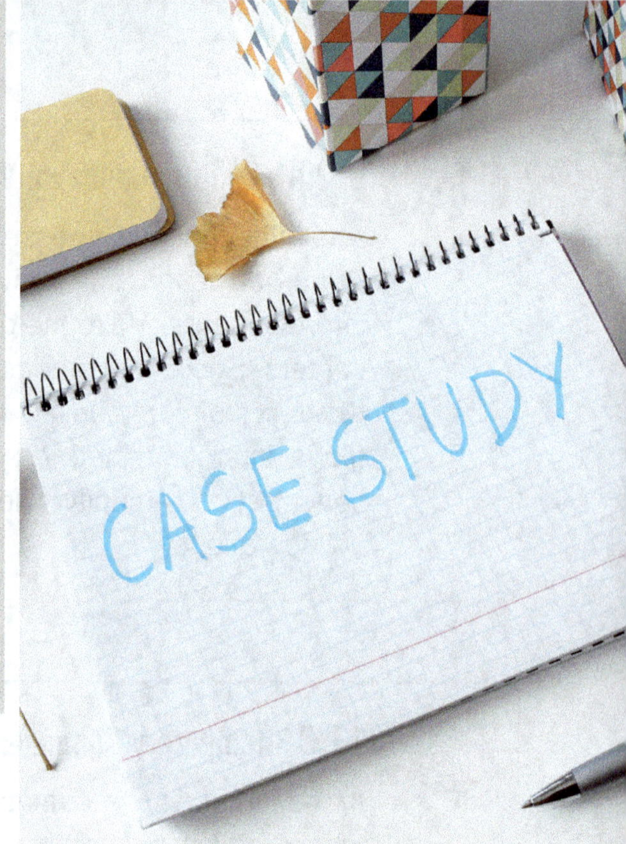

Emirates

The term "Emirates community" typically refers to the social and cultural fabric within the United Arab Emirates (UAE).

As a federation of seven emirates located on the Arabian Peninsula, the UAE boasts a rich and diverse community shaped by a unique blend of tradition, modernity, and globalization.

1. Cultural Diversity:

The Emirates community is inherently diverse, with each emirate maintaining its distinct cultural identity. Abu Dhabi, Dubai, Sharjah, Ajman, Umm Al-Quwain, Fujairah, and Ras Al Khaimah contribute to the mosaic of traditions, languages, and customs. The cultural diversity is further enriched by the presence of a large expatriate population, creating a cosmopolitan atmosphere that is a hallmark of UAE society.

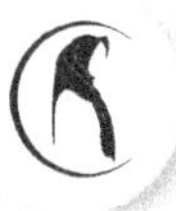

2. Islamic Traditions:

Islam plays a central role in the Emirates community, influencing both social and legal aspects of life. The majority of the population adheres to Sunni Islam, and Islamic traditions permeate various facets of daily life, including family dynamics, celebrations, and community interactions. Mosques serve as not only places of worship but also community hubs.

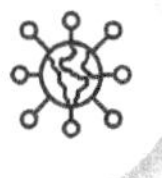

3. Modern Urban Centers:

The UAE is renowned for its modern and cosmopolitan cities, with Dubai and Abu Dhabi standing out as global hubs for business, tourism, and innovation. These urban centers have attracted a diverse expatriate population, contributing to a dynamic and forward-thinking community that embraces technological advancements and modern lifestyles.

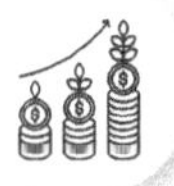

4. Economic Prosperity:

The UAE is the second largest economy in the Arab world, following Saudi Arabia. In 2018, its GDP was $414 billion (AED 1.52 trillion), and a third of that came from oil revenues. The economy was expected to grow between 4% and 4.5% in 2013, compared to 2.3% to 3.5% in the previous five years. Since gaining independence in 1971, the UAE's economy has grown almost 231 times to reach AED 1.45 trillion in 2013. Non-oil trade increased to AED 1.2 trillion, growing about 28 times from 1981 to 2012.

The UAE's economy is highly open globally, with a history dating back to times when ships sailed to India along the Swahili coast, reaching as far south as Mozambique. The UAE ranks among the top 20 for global service business, in the top 30 on the WEF's "most-networked countries," and is in the top quarter as one of the least corrupt countries according to TI's corruption index.

In response to economic shocks from the prolonged coronavirus lockdown, the government of the United Arab Emirates announced a broad restructuring and merger of over 50% of its federal agencies, including ministries and departments.

5. Family Values:

Family holds paramount importance in the Emirates community. Strong familial bonds, respect for elders, and a sense of collective responsibility characterize the social fabric. Traditional family values coexist with modern lifestyles, creating a balance that underpins social cohesion and stability.

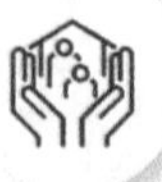

6. Community Initiatives:

The UAE government actively promotes community initiatives to enhance the well-being of its residents. Programs related to social welfare, health, and affordable housing aim to create a thriving and inclusive society. The leadership's commitment to community development reinforces the notion of the UAE as a nation that values the welfare and happiness of its residents.

Chinese Community

The Chinese community is a varied and widespread group worldwide, including people of Chinese background with strong cultural, historical, and language connections. This community has made important contributions in different areas, like business, technology, art, and philosophy. To grasp the Chinese community, we need to look at its history, culture, spread, and what's happening today.

1. Historical Roots:

The Chinese community's history goes way back to China's ancient civilization, which is thousands of years old. China has a long and interesting history with dynasties, philosophies, and cool inventions, and all of that has played a big part in shaping the Chinese community and its culture.

2. Diaspora and Global Presence:

People from China moving to different places around the globe has led to the creation of big and powerful Chinese communities around the world. Chinese immigrants with the help of their motherland have created communities in Africa, Southeast Asia, North America, Europe, and Oceania. This movement has been super important in making economic connections, sharing cultures, and linking the world together.

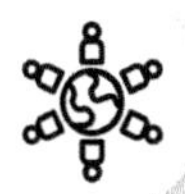

3. Cultural Diversity:

The Chinese community has lots of differences, like different groups, languages, and speaking styles. The largest group is the Han Chinese, but there are also many smaller groups with their own unique cultural traditions. You can see the diversity in the Chinese community through the languages they use, the food they enjoy, and the customs they have.

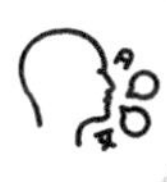

4. Language and Literature:

The Chinese language, predominantly Mandarin, is a unifying factor within the community. The Chinese writing system, composed of characters, has a rich literary tradition spanning classical poetry, philosophy, and modern literature. The promotion of Chinese language and literature remains a key aspect of cultural preservation and identity.

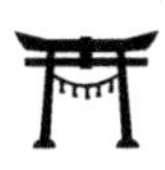

5. Philosophical Traditions:

Chinese philosophical traditions, such as Confucianism, Daoism, and Buddhism, have profoundly influenced the Chinese community's values, ethics, and worldview. These philosophies emphasize harmony, respect for elders, and the pursuit of moral virtues, shaping the cultural ethos of the community.

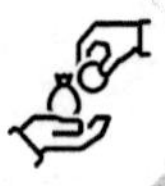

6. Economy Contributions

China plays a crucial role in today's global economy. It has experienced rapid economic growth, adopted innovative strategies, and gained global influence, evolving from a regional to a global economic leader. Through active participation in international organizations, extensive trade networks, and investments in global infrastructure projects, China significantly impacts the world economic system. China's sustained economic progress, contributing approximately 30 percent to global economic growth, makes it a vital engine for worldwide development. In 2023, China exceeded its GDP growth target of 5 percent, achieving a revival with 5.2 percent growth..

The Belt and Road Initiative, celebrating its 10th anniversary in 2023, is one of China's ambitious global economic projects. The initiative's third international cooperation forum achieved 458 significant outcomes, with Chinese financial institutions allocating $109.23 billion to associated projects. China's transportation infrastructure, including air connections with over 100 countries and a substantial maritime fleet, plays a critical role in its economic dominance. China's industry holds a significant influence globally, leading in various sectors and maintaining the world's top position in industrial added value for 14 consecutive years. With over 200 major industrial clusters, China contributes to the global distribution of production factors and enhances worldwide productivity.

Initiatives like the South-South Cooperation Assistance Fund, with a capital of $4 billion, and the preparation for a $10 billion special fund by Chinese financial institutions highlight China's strategic role in supporting international development and strengthening global partnerships. Foreign investments in China saw a substantial increase, with 41,947 enterprises with foreign investments established in the first nine months of 2023, reflecting the attractiveness of the Chinese market to international investors.

7. Education and Innovation:

Education is highly valued within the Chinese community, reflecting Confucian traditions that emphasize the pursuit of knowledge. Chinese communities worldwide have produced notable scholars, scientists, and innovators. The emphasis on education contributes to a strong work ethic and a commitment to excellence.

The Jewish Community

The Jewish community is a diverse and resilient global entity with a rich history, cultural heritage, and profound impact on various aspects of human civilization. There are few things that we shall be looking at if we want to understand the jewish community.

1. Ancient Origins:

The history of the Jewish community dates back thousands of years to the ancient Middle East. The foundational texts of Judaism, including the Torah and Talmud, contain narratives of patriarchs, matriarchs, and the establishment of a covenant with God. The Hebrew Bible chronicles the journey of the Israelites, from slavery in Egypt to the Promised Land.

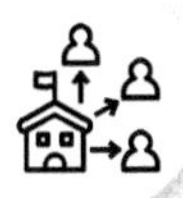

2. Diaspora and Dispersion:

The dispersion of the Jewish people, known as the Diaspora, began with the Babylonian exile in the 6th century BCE. Throughout history, Jews migrated and established communities in various regions, including Europe, North Africa, the Middle East, and eventually the Americas. The Diaspora has been a defining aspect of Jewish history, contributing to cultural diversity and adaptation.

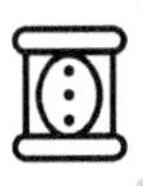

3. Cultural Traditions:

The Jewish community has many cultural traditions that make it special. Doing religious things, following customs, and doing rituals are important parts of being Jewish. Celebrations like Shabbat, Passover, Rosh Hashanah, Yom Kippur, and Hanukkah are examples of important times that connect people and keep their shared heritage going.

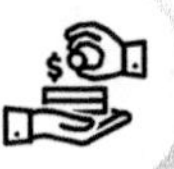

4. Intellectual Contributions:

The Jewish community has made substantial intellectual contributions to various fields. Historically, Jewish scholars played key roles in preserving and transmitting knowledge during the Middle Ages, contributing to fields such as philosophy, medicine, and mathematics. In modern times, Jewish individuals have excelled in science, literature, music, and the arts.

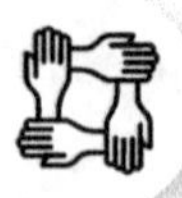

5. Religious Diversity:

Within the Jewish community, there exists religious diversity encompassing various denominations such as Orthodox, Conservative, Reform, and Reconstructionist Judaism. Each denomination interprets religious texts and practices differently, contributing to a dynamic spectrum of religious observance and belief systems.

6. Community Organizations and Institutions:

The Jewish community is characterized by a network of organizations and institutions that play vital roles in education, social welfare, and cultural preservation. Synagogues, schools, Jewish community centers, and philanthropic organizations contribute to community cohesion and engagement.

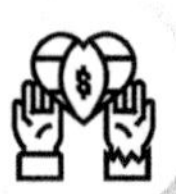

7. Jewish Contributions to Society:

Jews have made significant contributions to various fields, including science, medicine, literature, entertainment, and business. Notable individuals such as Albert Einstein, Sigmund Freud, Leonard Bernstein, and many others have left a significant mark on human achievement, reflecting the diversity and talent within the Jewish community.

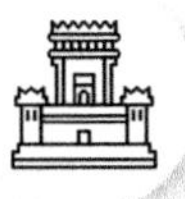

8. Wealth In The Jewish Community:

Let's look at the Jewish community in America as an example. Since massive immigration around 100 years ago, Jews have become the wealthiest religious group in American society, comprising only 2% of the population but constituting 25% of the 400 wealthiest Americans. The aid provided by influential figures like World Jewish Congress President Ronald Lauder plays a crucial role.

Lauder, a billionaire with an estimated wealth of $2.7 billion, is a significant contributor to numerous Jewish and Israeli organizations. Examining the broader context, many Israeli adults received support from "the rich uncle in America" during their childhood. Various organizations in Israel, including hospitals and universities, benefit from billions in donations from the United States. A study by Hebrew University indicates that these donations make up about two-thirds of all contributions in Israel. The Jewish Encyclopedia notes that around 5.6 million Jews reside in the United States, making up 1.8% of the population.

Notably, Jews are concentrated in affluent cities such as Miami, Los Angeles, Philadelphia, Boston, and primarily New York. Research from the Pew Forum in 2008 reveals that Jews are the wealthiest religious group in the U.S., with 46% earning over $100,000 a year, compared to 19% of the general population. Beyond individual wealth, over 100 of the 400 billionaires on Forbes' list in America are Jewish. Jews also hold a significant presence in Wall Street, Silicon Valley, the U.S. Congress and Administration, Hollywood, TV networks, and the American press, exceeding their percentage in the population.

The success of American Jews becomes more remarkable when considering their history. Initially, only a few thousand Jews lived in the U.S. at its establishment in 1776, but a significant wave of immigration started in 1882, making the U.S. the largest Jewish concentration globally. Despite facing challenges, including anti-Semitic campaigns and limited job opportunities, Jews rose from poverty, contributing to labor unions and gaining professional success. Anti-Semitism weakened after World War II, and Jews gradually integrated into American society, moving from slums to suburbs. The success of Jewish immigrants is attributed to factors like education and mutual support within the community. The Jewish communal organization is considered a role model for other ethnic groups, providing assistance and equal opportunities.

White South African Community

White South Africans are a varied group with a complicated history that's closely connected to the nation's overall story. Even though they're a minority, the white population has had a big impact on how South Africa's culture, economy, and politics have developed.

1. Historical Context:

The history of the White South African community is closely tied to South Africa's overall history, including colonialism, apartheid, and what came after. European settlers, mostly from Dutch and British backgrounds, came in the 17th century and set up the Dutch Cape Colony. As time passed, this community expanded and turned into the Afrikaner and English-speaking groups.

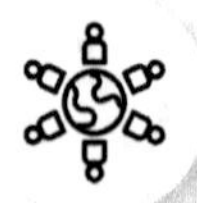

2. Cultural Diversity:

The White South African community is diverse, made up of different ethnic, language, and cultural groups. The Afrikaner community, with its Dutch and Huguenot roots, has its own cultural traditions, like the Afrikaans language, literature, and religious practices. English-speaking South Africans, usually of British descent, add to the cultural mix by combining British traditions with local influences.

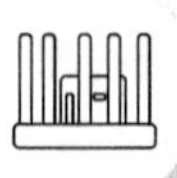

3. Apartheid Era:

A defining chapter in the history of the White South African community is the era of apartheid, a system of institutionalized racial segregation and discrimination enforced by the National Party government from 1948 to 1994. The policy affected all South Africans but had profound implications for the white population, shaping their perceptions, attitudes, and experiences.

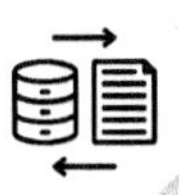

4. Challenges and Transformations:

The end of apartheid ushered in a period of significant change and challenges for the White South African community. Political reforms, truth and reconciliation initiatives, and efforts towards social integration presented both opportunities and difficulties. Adjusting to a new political landscape required the community to confront historical injustices and engage in processes of reconciliation.

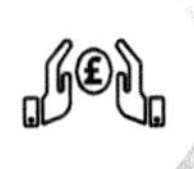

5. Economic Contributions:

White South Africans, on average, tended to have higher incomes compared to their counterparts. However, post-apartheid South Africa has undertaken measures to address these imbalances, aiming for more inclusive economic growth. The White South Africans are split into Afrikaans-speaking descendants of Dutch East India Company settlers, known as Afrikaners, and English-speaking descendants of British colonists.

South Africa's progress in well-being has stalled since the mid-1990s. Poverty decreased from 68% (2005) to 56% (2010) but rose to 57% (2015) and projected 60% (2020). Structural challenges and weak growth worsened due to COVID-19. Unemployment peaked at 35.3% (Q4 2021) and slightly declined to 32.6% (Q2 2023), with youth unemployment at 61%.

A tweet claims there are 1.8 million white and 30 million black working-age people in South Africa, but this is underestimated. The country has 40.2 million working-age individuals, with 2.84 million (7%) categorized as white and 37.3 million (93%) as black. It's mostly correct, though imprecise, that the private sector has a yearly turnover of around R10 trillion, while the government's annual budget is just R2 trillion. A viral tweet from October 2022 presents surprising figures about race and ownership in South Africa's private sector. It alleges that 1.8 million white working-age people control "over 90%" of the country's R10 trillion private sector, while 30 million "natives" contend for a share of the R2 trillion government budget. Similar claims have circulated for years. In 2017, former president Jacob Zuma stated that only 10% of top companies on the main stock exchange were owned by black South Africans.

6. Identity and Heritage:

White South Africans grapple with questions of identity and heritage, navigating a complex landscape shaped by historical legacies and contemporary realities. For some, there is a connection to Afrikaner nationalism and cultural preservation, while others embrace a more inclusive South African identity that transcends racial lines.

7. Language and Education:

Language has been a significant aspect of the White South African community's identity. Afrikaans and English are both widely spoken, reflecting historical divisions. The educational landscape has undergone changes to promote inclusivity and address historical inequalities, with efforts to diversify curriculum content and increase access to quality education.

8. Social Integration and Challenges:

Post-apartheid South Africa has seen ongoing efforts towards social integration, aiming to break down racial barriers and foster a more inclusive society. However, challenges persist, including social inequalities, cultural divisions, and the need for continued dialogue and understanding between different communities.

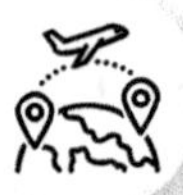

9. Diaspora Connections:

The White South African community has experienced diaspora movements, with some individuals choosing to emigrate for various reasons, including economic opportunities, safety concerns, or a desire for a different social and political environment. The diaspora community maintains ties to South Africa, contributing to transnational connections.

Freemasons Community

Freemasonry, a really old secret group with symbols and special ceremonies, has fascinated a lot of people. We want to look into the history, principles, rituals, and influence of the Freemasons, trying to explain this ancient community.

1. Origins and Historical Roots:

Freemasonry's origins are steeped in antiquity, with its roots tracing back to medieval stonemason guilds in Europe. The exact origins remain elusive, but the establishment of the Grand Lodge of England in 1717 marked a pivotal moment in the formalization of modern Freemasonry. The fraternity's symbols and rituals draw inspiration from the practices of medieval stonemasons and the Enlightenment era.

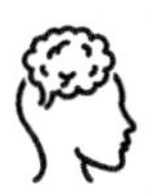

2. Principles and Ideals:

Central to Freemasonry are its principles and ideals, encapsulated in a set of moral and ethical teachings. Freemasons are guided by core tenets such as brotherly love, relief, and truth. The fraternity places a strong emphasis on personal development, moral integrity, and contributing to the well-being of society.

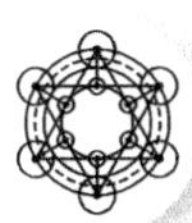

3. Masonic Symbolism:

Freemasonry is known for using a lot of symbols in its rituals and buildings. Some well-known symbols, like the square and compass, the all-seeing eye, and the apron, have deep meanings in the Masonic tradition. These symbols are like tools to teach important moral and spiritual lessons.

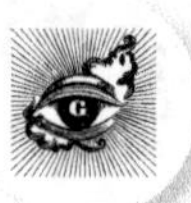

5. Freemasonry and Politics:

Freemasonry has, at times, been entwined with political narratives. Historical figures, including several U.S. Presidents, European monarchs, and influential thinkers, were Freemasons. However, the fraternity officially prohibits discussions of politics and religion within its lodges, emphasizing the importance of unity and diversity.

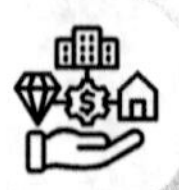

6. Freemasonry's wealth:

Freemasonry is often seen as a group encouraging personal growth, moral values, and community service. Some notable members like Benjamin Franklin, Henry Ford, Winston Churchill, George Washington, and Buzz Aldrin attribute their personal development to the principles and experiences gained within the organization.

As a Freemason, Franklin valued self-improvement and moral conduct promoted by the fraternity. His success as a polymath, statesman, and entrepreneur is influenced by the moral teachings and fellowship within Freemasonry. Ford, the founder of Ford Motor Company, was a Freemason who emphasized innovation and mass production. While his business success is attributed to these principles, Freemasonry contributed to his character development and ethical considerations in business.

Winston Churchill, the former Prime Minister of the United Kingdom was a Freemason and known for his leadership during World War II. While Churchill's leadership qualities were shaped by various factors, some Freemasons argue that the principles of leadership and integrity within the organization have influenced his statesmanship. These principles when adopted in different sectors of life such as business, education and others will certainly yield high productivity.

Patel Family

The Patel family, just like many other families who moved to the United States, has been important in making the culture, money, and how people live there. During this section, we will talk about the Patel family's history, their culture, what they've given to the U.S., and the hard parts they've dealt with. It helps us understand their experiences and how they've made a difference.

1. Immigration and Historical Context:

The Patel family's journey to the United States is part of a broader narrative of immigration. Historically, many Patel families emigrated from the Indian state of Gujarat, seeking opportunities and a better life in the land of possibilities. Their arrival spans several waves, from the mid-20th century to more recent years, contributing to the diversity of the Indian diaspora in the U.S.

2. Cultural Heritage:

The Patel family's cultural roots come from the lively traditions of Gujarat, India. They celebrate colorful festivals like Diwali and Navratri and enjoy tasty dishes like Dhokla and Thepla. These customs and practices from the Patels add to the mix of cultures in the United States.

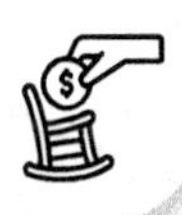

3. Economic Contributions and Entrepreneurship:

The Patel family played a big role in starting the Planning Commission of India. This group made plans for the country's development over five years. These plans focused on making sure all parts of the country grow together.

Patel liked the idea of giving power to local governments. This way, each region could solve its own problems and use its strengths for economic development.

Their legacy goes beyond what they did directly. Patels' dedication to the country's unity and economic growth laid the foundation for India becoming a strong and self-sufficient economy and one of the richest families in India and America.

4. Professional Diversity:

While many Patels have made their mark in the hospitality sector, the family is increasingly diversifying into various professional fields. From medicine and technology to academia and law, the Patels are breaking new ground and contributing to the professional landscape of the U.S. Their success stories inspire subsequent generations to pursue diverse career paths.

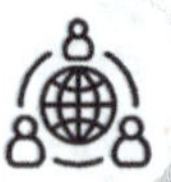

5. Community and Social Networks:

The Patel family's sense of community extends beyond familial ties to include broader social networks. Community and cultural organizations provide platforms for social interaction, support systems, and the preservation of cultural identity. These networks play a crucial role in maintaining a connection to their roots while navigating the dynamics of American society.

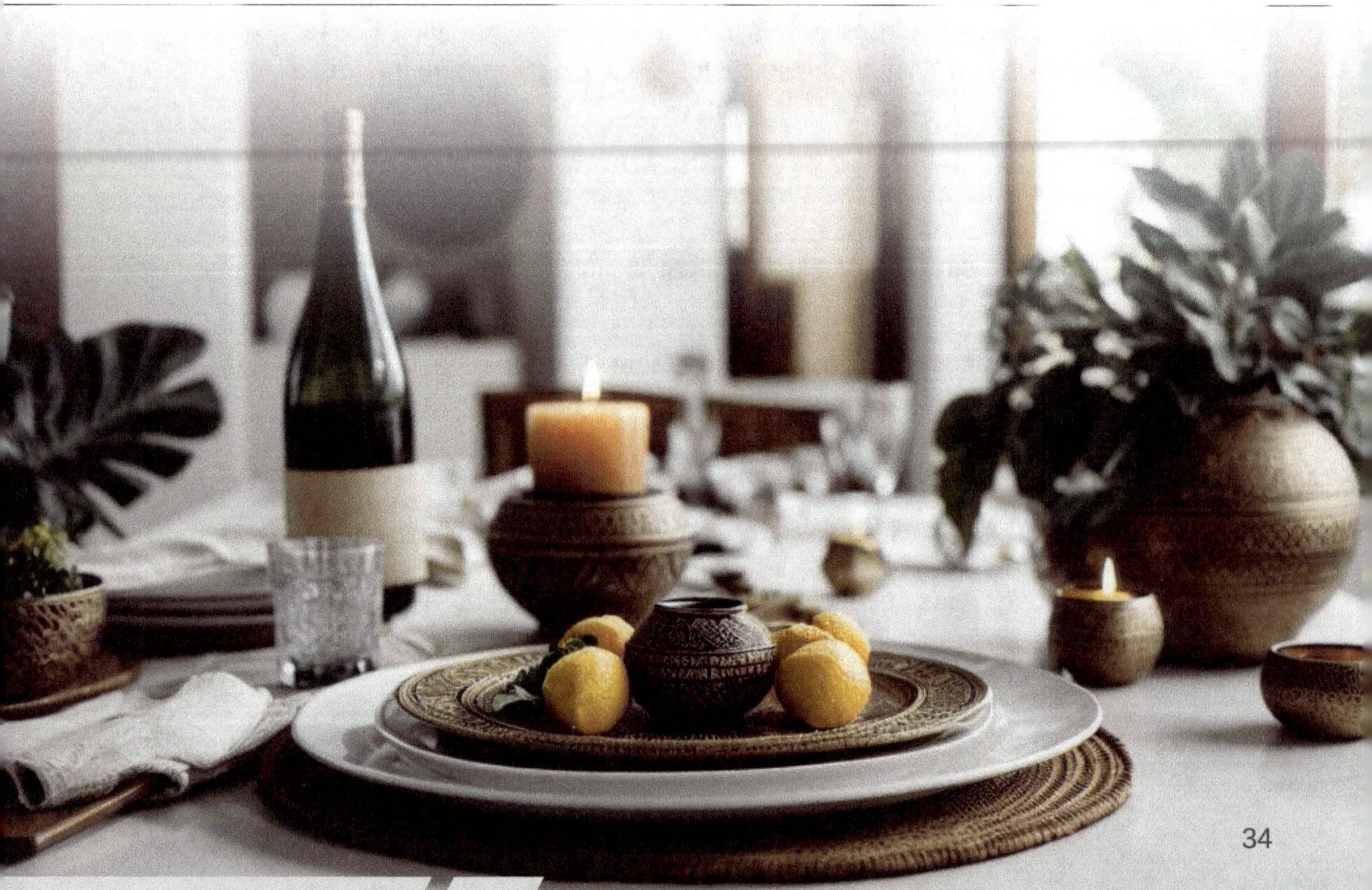

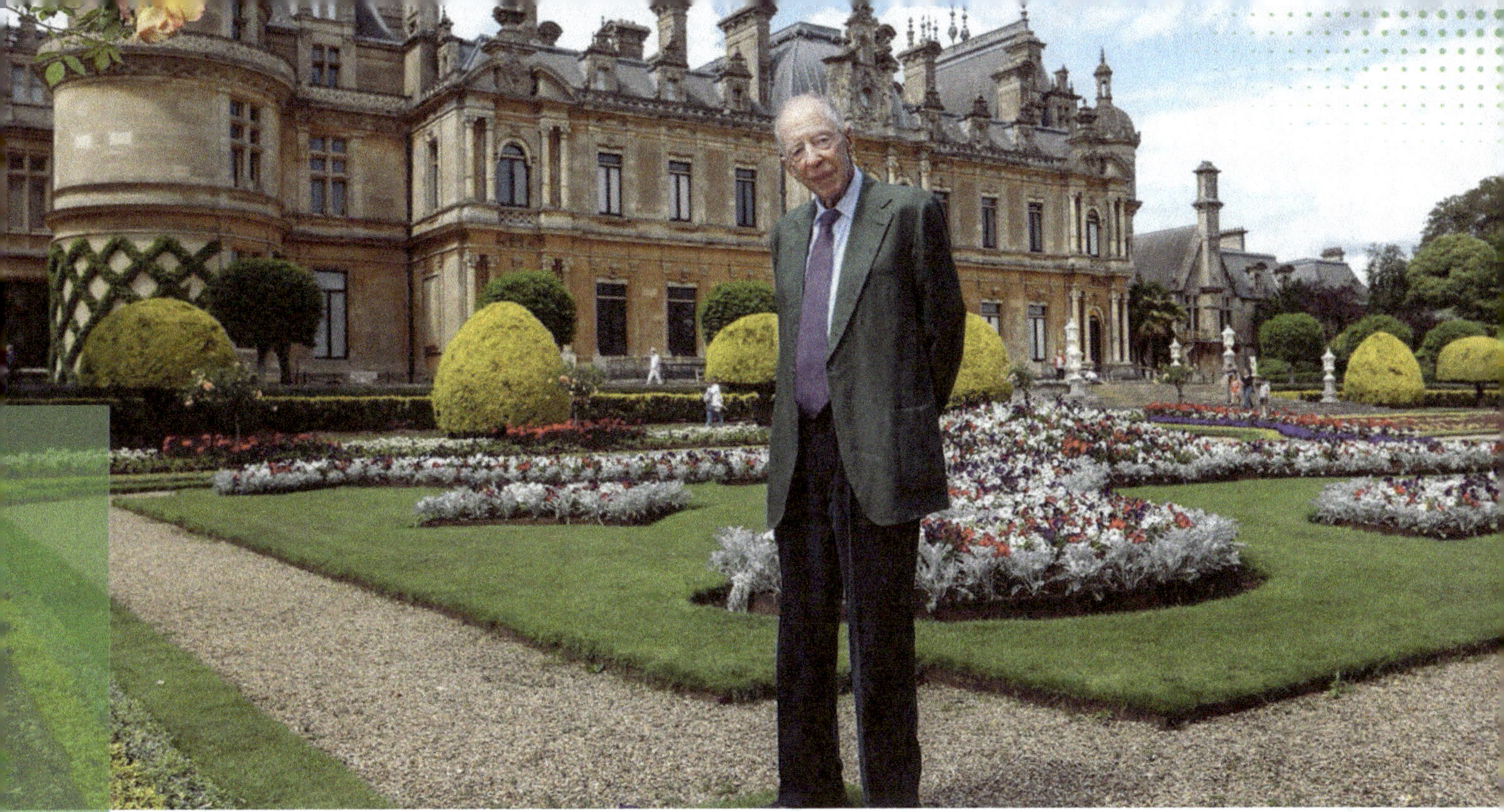

The Rothschild Family

The Rothschild family is a prominent and historically significant banking dynasty that originated in the late 18th century. Founded by Mayer Amschel Rothschild in Frankfurt, Germany, the family's success in finance and banking propelled them to international prominence. Over the years, the Rothschilds have been subject to various conspiracy theories and have played a crucial role in shaping global finance.

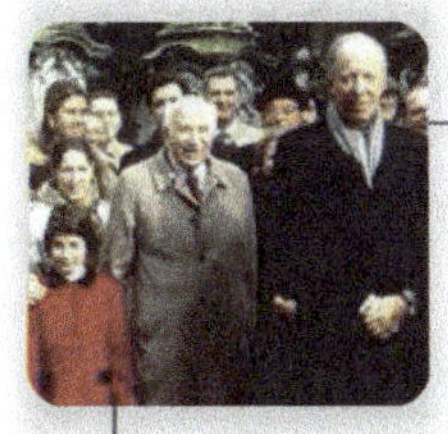

Founding and Early Years:

Mayer Amschel Rothschild, born in 1744, established a banking business in the late 18th century. His five sons, spread across major European financial centers – Frankfurt, London, Paris, Vienna, and Naples, expanded the family's banking operations. This decentralized structure allowed them to capitalize on emerging financial markets across Europe.

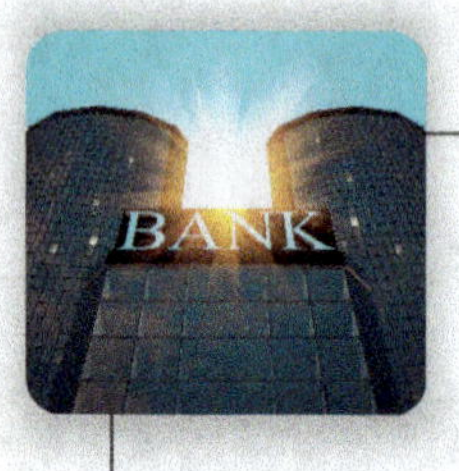

Banking Empire:

The Rothschild banking empire grew rapidly, with each son managing a branch in different cities. They facilitated international trade and financed infrastructure projects, playing a vital role in the economic development of various European nations. Their reputation for trustworthiness and financial acumen attracted clients ranging from royalty to industrialists.

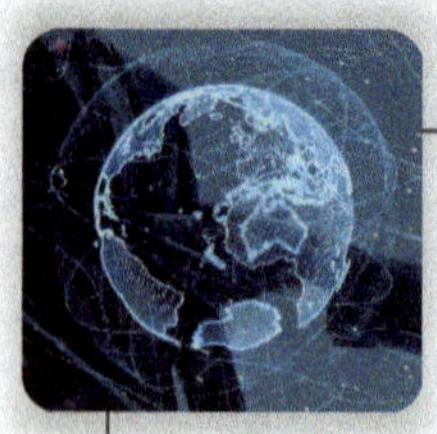

Modern Era:

In the modern era, the Rothschild family continues to be involved in various business ventures. However, the family's influence in global finance has diminished compared to its peak in the 19th century. The banking industry has undergone significant transformations, and the Rothschilds have adapted to these changes.

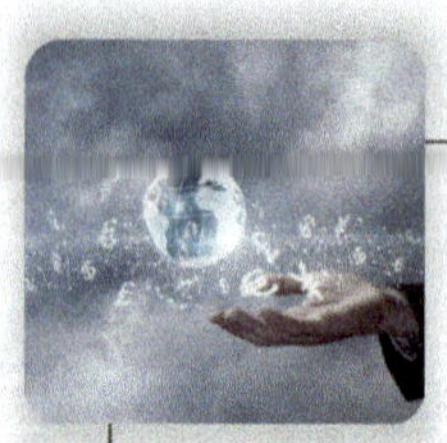

Legacy and Impact

The Rothschild family's legacy is marked by their pioneering role in international finance, their contributions to economic development, and their enduring philanthropic endeavors. While the family's influence may have waned in certain aspects, their impact on the history of banking and finance remains notable.

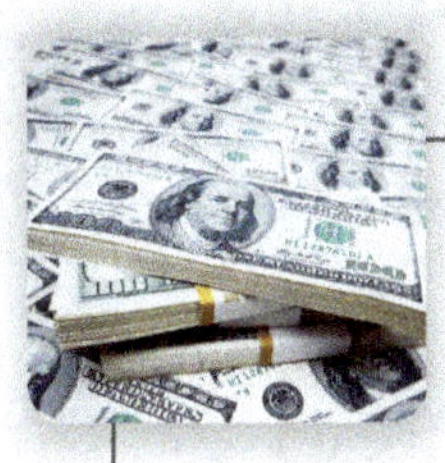

Rothschild's Wealth

Since 2003, a group of Rothschild banks has been controlled by Rothschild Continuation Holdings with over 14 billion Euros in assets under management. Rothschild Continuation Holdings, a Swiss holding company chaired by Baron David René de Rothschild and over 2,000 employees.

N M Rothschild & Sons, an English investment bank, specializes in mergers and acquisitions advice. In 2004, it withdrew from the gold market, and in 2006, it ranked second in UK M&A with deals totaling $104.9 billion, recording a pre-tax annual profit of £83.2 million. The Rockefeller family expressed a strong connection between the two families. In 1991, Jacob Rothschild founded J. Rothschild Assurance Group, now St. James's Place Wealth Management. In 2001, the Rothschild mansion in London was listed for £85 million, and in 2009, Jacob Rothschild invested $200 million in a North Sea oil company.

In 2010, Nathaniel Philip Rothschild acquired a substantial share of Glencore mining and oil company's market capitalization and a large share of United Company RUSAL. The Rothschilds controlled the Rio Tinto mining corporation in the 19th century, maintaining a close business relationship. The Rothschild family has been in winemaking for 150 years, owning estates across France and globally. Notably, Château Mouton Rothschild and Château Lafite Rothschild are classified as Premier Cru Classé. Saskia de Rothschild chairs Château Lafite Rothschild, and Château Mouton Rothschild is directed by Philippe Sereys de Rothschild since 2014.

The family, known for one of the largest private art collections globally, made significant art donations to public museums, sometimes anonymously. In 2014, Hannah Mary Rothschild became the chair of the board of the National Gallery of London.

The European Community / European Union

The European Union (EU) is a political and economic
union of member states, primarily located in Europe.

Originating from post-World War II cooperation, the
EU has evolved into a unique entity with profound
implications for its member nations and the broader
international community.

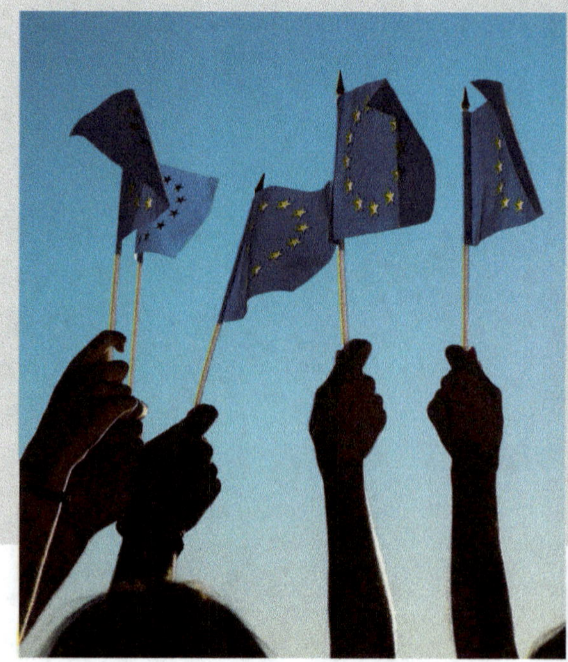

Historical Foundations:

The roots of the EU can be traced back to the aftermath of World War II, with the aim of
fostering economic cooperation and preventing future conflicts. The European Coal and
Steel Community (ECSC) was established in 1951, marking the first step towards European
integration. The Treaty of Rome in 1957 expanded this collaboration into the European
Economic Community (EEC).

Expansion and Integration:

Over the years, the EU has expanded both geographically and in terms of its competencies.
The accession of new member states, from the original six to the current 27, has
strengthened the union's diversity. Additionally, various treaties, including the Maastricht
Treaty in 1992, have deepened integration, leading to the establishment of the Eurozone
and the introduction of the euro currency.

Institutions and Decision-Making:

The EU operates through a complex system of institutions, each with specific roles. The
European Commission, European Parliament, Council of the European Union, and the
European Council form the core decision-making bodies. The Commission, as the executive
branch, proposes legislation, while the Parliament and Council deliberate and adopt laws.
The European Court of Justice ensures the interpretation and application of EU law.

Single Market and Customs Union:

One of the EU's fundamental achievements is the creation of a single market, eliminating barriers to the free movement of goods, services, capital, and people. The customs union facilitates seamless trade within the EU, contributing to economic growth and cooperation. The Schengen Area, allowing passport-free travel across many member states, further enhances integration.

Common Foreign and Security Policy:

The EU pursues a common foreign and security policy to promote stability and cooperation globally. While member states retain control over certain aspects of foreign policy, the EU works towards a unified approach on various international issues, including diplomacy, conflict resolution, and humanitarian efforts.

Challenges and Criticisms:

Despite its successes, the EU faces challenges and criticisms. Issues such as the democratic deficit, where decision-making power is perceived to be distant from citizens, have been raised. The handling of economic crises, migration, and concerns about sovereignty have fueled debates about the EU's future direction.

Enlargement and Neighborhood Policy:

Enlargement has been a key aspect of the EU's evolution. The prospect of joining the union has motivated reforms in candidate countries, fostering stability and democratic governance. Additionally, the EU's neighborhood policy aims to strengthen relations with neighboring countries, promoting cooperation and stability in the broader European region.

Brexit and its Implications:

The United Kingdom's decision to leave the EU, commonly known as Brexit, marked a significant moment in the union's history. The intricate negotiations and the subsequent agreement highlighted the complexities of disentangling a member state from the EU framework, with repercussions for both parties.

Future Prospects:

The EU continues to adapt to new challenges, including global economic shifts, technological advancements, and geopolitical uncertainties. Discussions about further integration, a stronger common defense policy, and addressing environmental concerns reflect the ongoing evolution of the union.

The economy of The European Union & European Community:

The twelve new countries in the European Union had higher economic growth than the older members. Slovakia had the highest GDP growth from 2005 to 2015. The Baltic states, especially Latvia, achieved significant growth, comparable to China. This growth was due to stable monetary policies, export-focused trade, low flat taxes, and using affordable labor. In 2015, Ireland had the EU's highest GDP growth at 25.1%. The EU's growth pattern varies, with larger economies facing slow growth, while newer states experience strong economic growth.

In mid-2021, the EU's gross saving rate was 18%, up from the pre-COVID-19 average of 11–13%. During Q2 2020, families' primary income dropped by 7.3%, but secondary income increased by 6.5%. As of September 2018, the EU's adjusted unemployment rate was 6.7%, with the euro area at 8.1%.

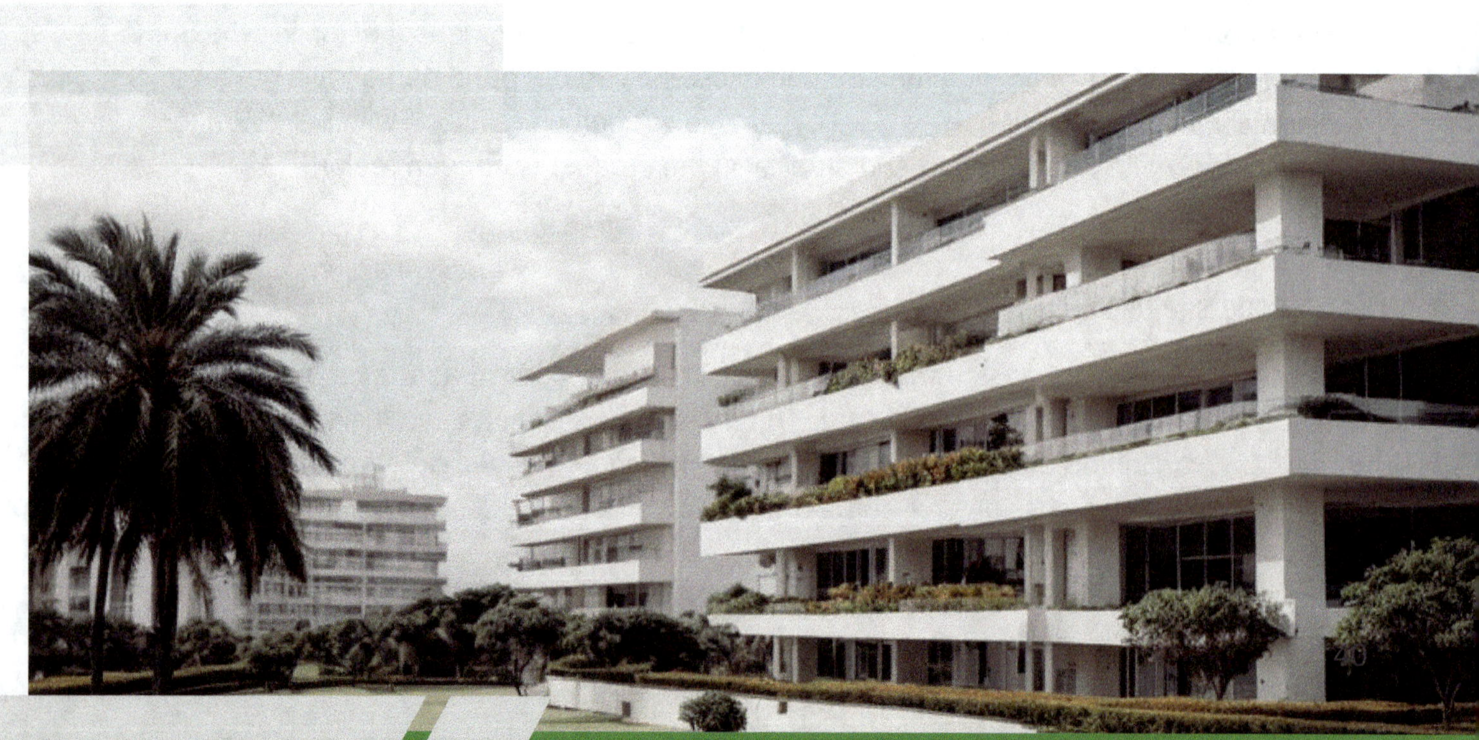

Mondragon Cooperatives

The Mondragon Cooperatives, located in the Basque region of Spain, stand as a remarkable example of cooperative economic and social organization. Founded in 1956 by a visionary priest, Father José María Arizmendiarrieta, the Mondragon Cooperatives have grown into a network of worker-owned enterprises that spans various industries.

Origins and Founding:

The story of the Mondragon Cooperatives begins in the aftermath of the Spanish Civil War, a time of economic hardship and social upheaval. Father Arizmendiarrieta, inspired by the principles of Catholic social teaching and cooperative movements, sought to address the economic challenges facing the community of Mondragon. His vision was to create a cooperative network that prioritized the well-being of its members.

Cooperative Principles:

At the heart of the Mondragon model are the principles of worker ownership, participatory decision-making, solidarity, and social responsibility. Each cooperative within the Mondragon network is owned and governed by its workers, who actively participate in the decision-making processes. This democratic structure ensures that the interests of the workers are central to the cooperative's operations.

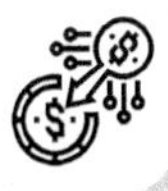

Diversified Industries:

The Mondragon Cooperatives have expanded across a diverse range of industries, including manufacturing, finance, education, and research. The federation encompasses over 250 enterprises, employing tens of thousands of individuals. This diversification has contributed to the resilience of the Mondragon model, allowing it to adapt to economic changes and challenges.

Education and Training:

A crucial aspect of the Mondragon approach is its emphasis on education and training. The Mondragon Cooperative Experience, an educational program, imparts cooperative values and business skills to its members. This commitment to continuous learning fosters a sense of ownership and responsibility among the workers.

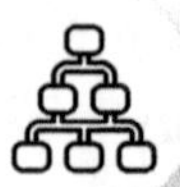

Financial Structure:

The financial structure of the Mondragon Cooperatives includes a cooperative bank, Caja Laboral, providing financial services to its members. This banking component supports the cooperatives in securing capital, managing finances, and investing in new ventures. The cooperative bank aligns with the overall cooperative philosophy, reinforcing the self-sufficiency and autonomy of the Mondragon network.

Social Welfare and Solidarity:

The Mondragon model places a strong emphasis on social welfare and solidarity. The cooperatives prioritize job security, fair wages, and social benefits for their members. In times of economic hardship, there is a commitment to avoid layoffs, and efforts are made to redistribute work among the members. This focus on social responsibility distinguishes the Mondragon Cooperatives from traditional business models.

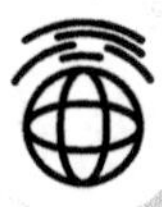

Global Influence and Inspiration:

The Mondragon Cooperatives have gained international recognition and have inspired cooperative movements worldwide. The model has been studied and emulated in various countries, contributing to the discourse on alternative economic systems that prioritize worker empowerment and social responsibility.

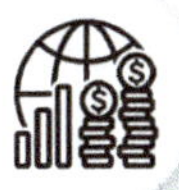

Mondragon's Economy

Mondragon is a leading company in casting iron and aluminum. In 2009, its Industrial Components sector had a turnover of €1.5 billion, serving as a supplier for car manufacturers and producing various vehicle components. In construction, sales reached €974 million in 2009, with Mondragon involved in building projects and supplying construction-related solutions. Services to business accounted for €248 million in 2008, offering consultancy, architecture, engineering, and other services. In 2013, 71.1% of turnover came from international sales, with subsidiaries in multiple countries. Mondragon also operates in retail through Eroski, a prominent group in Spain and southern France, with a turnover of €6.6 billion in 2013. Mondragon's knowledge sector focuses on education, training, and innovation, with Mondragon University playing a crucial role. The corporation is actively involved in technological innovation through R&D departments, technology centers, and the Garaia Innovation Park.

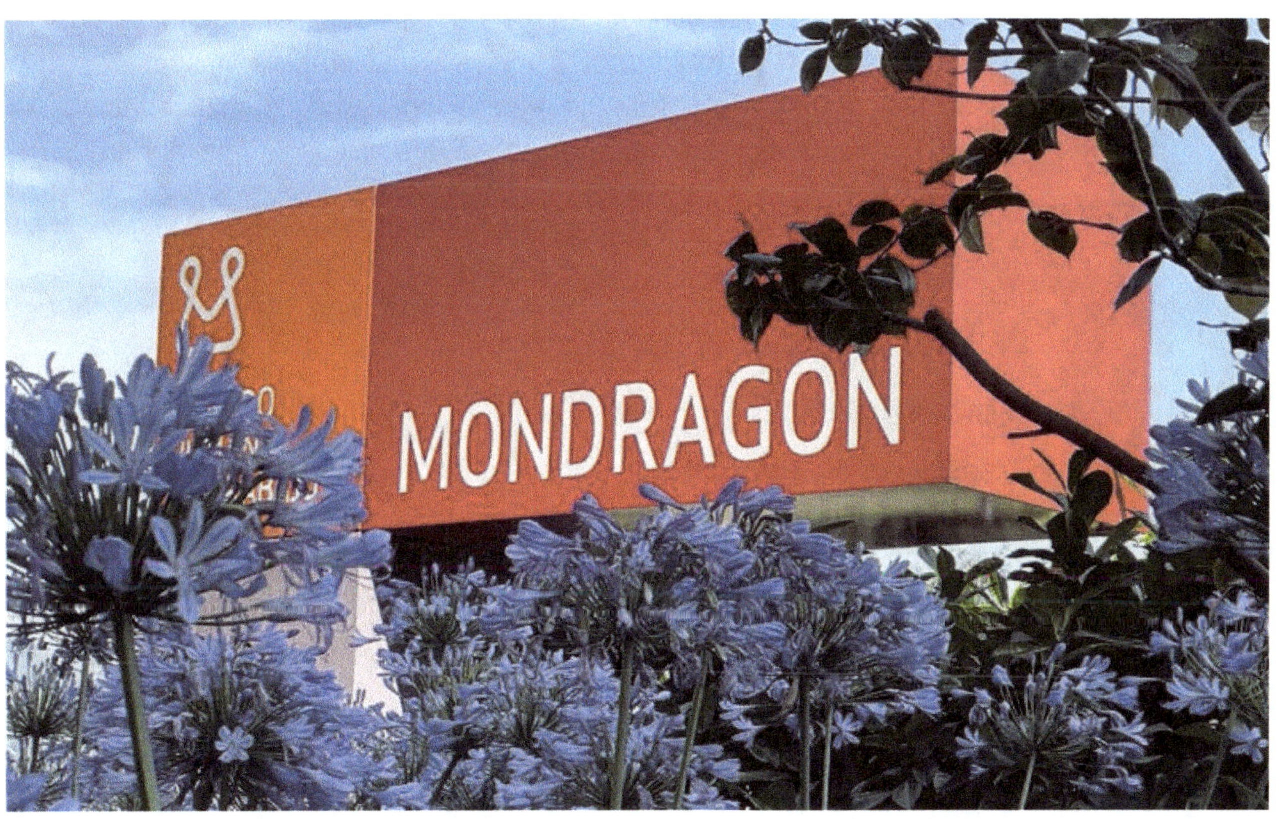

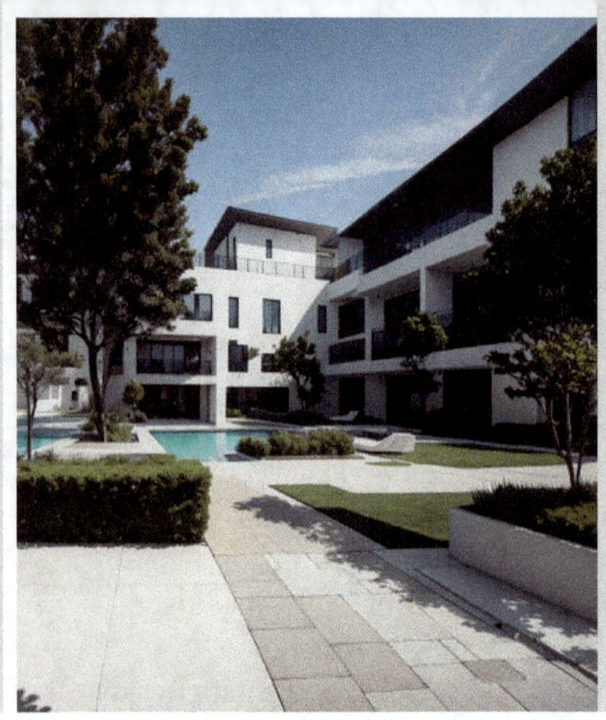

Professional Associations

Professional associations play a crucial role in bringing together individuals within specific industries or fields of expertise. These communities serve as platforms for networking, knowledge-sharing, and professional development.

The structure and functions of professional associations vary across different sectors, but they commonly aim to enhance the skills, knowledge, and collaboration among their members.

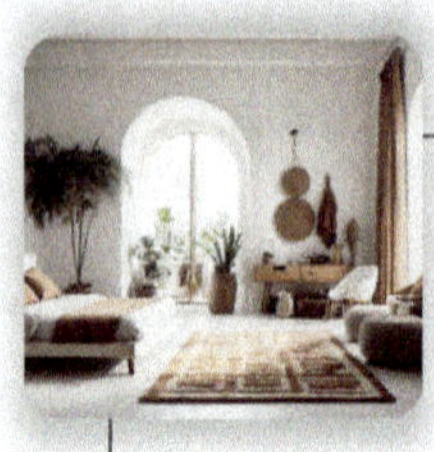

Formation and Purpose:

Professional associations are typically formed by individuals within a particular profession or industry seeking a collective voice. These organizations serve diverse purposes, including advocating for industry standards, providing continuing education opportunities, and fostering a sense of community among professionals. The formation of such associations often arises from the recognition of shared challenges, the need for collaboration, and a desire to elevate professional standards.

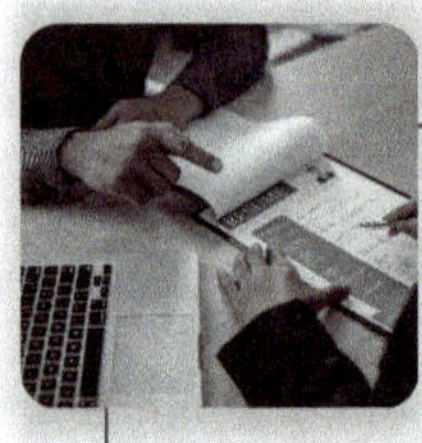

Membership Benefits:

Members of professional associations enjoy a range of benefits tailored to their specific needs. These may include access to industry-specific resources, networking events, professional development opportunities, and publications. Many associations also offer certification programs, recognizing members who meet certain standards of expertise or experience.

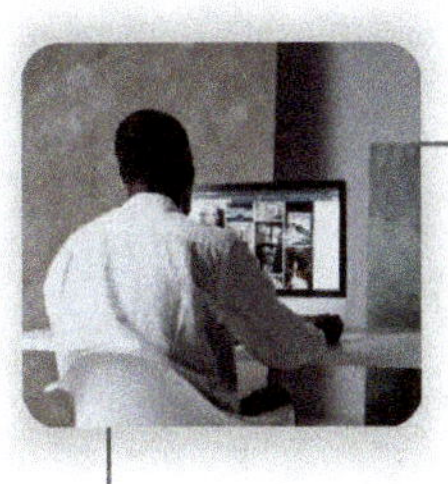

Networking Opportunities:

One of the primary functions of professional associations is to facilitate networking among members. Networking events, conferences, and online platforms provide professionals with opportunities to connect, share insights, and build valuable relationships. These interactions can lead to job opportunities, mentorship arrangements, and collaborative ventures.

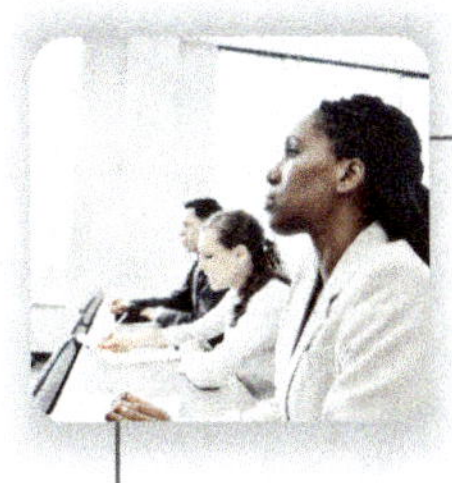

Continuing Education:

Professional development is a cornerstone of many associations. Through workshops, seminars, webinars, and conferences, members have access to ongoing education in their respective fields. This not only ensures that professionals stay abreast of the latest industry trends and technologies but also helps maintain high standards within the profession.

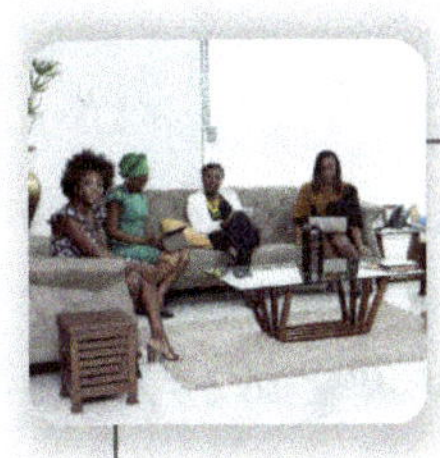

Diversity and Inclusion Initiatives:

In recent years, there has been a growing emphasis on diversity and inclusion within professional associations. Many organizations are actively working to ensure that their membership reflects a broad spectrum of backgrounds and experiences. Diversity initiatives aim to create a more inclusive professional community and foster a richer exchange of ideas.

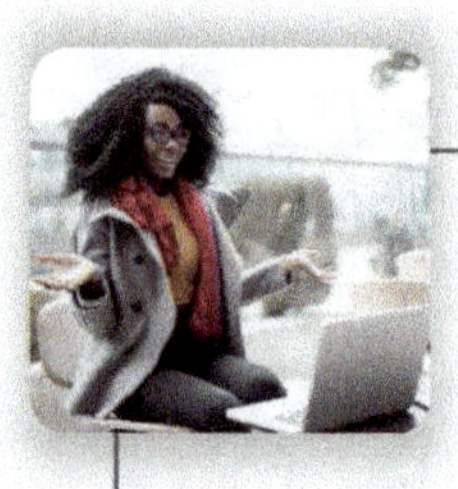

Technology and Online Communities:

Advancements in technology have significantly impacted professional associations. Online platforms and social media enable members to connect and collaborate irrespective of geographical distances. Virtual events and webinars have become integral parts of professional development, providing members with accessible and flexible learning opportunities.

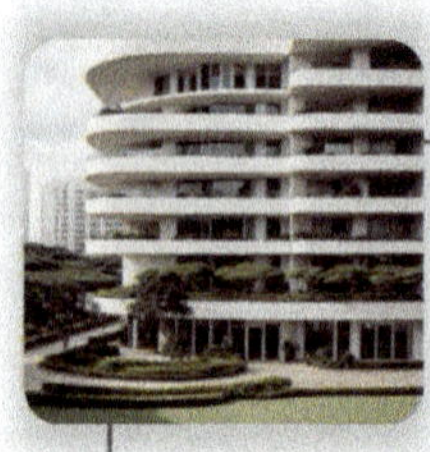

Global Influence:

Many professional associations extend their reach globally, collaborating with similar organizations worldwide. This global network allows professionals to gain insights into international best practices, fosters cross-cultural collaboration, and facilitates the exchange of knowledge on a global scale.

Economics of a member of an association / union VS non-member:

Unions offer a benefit called the "union wage premium," meaning union members earn more than non-members. Comparing wages, union workers typically make about 20% more than nonunion workers. Economists use different analyses to study unions' effects on wages, finding a 10-15% union wage premium, especially for longer-tenured workers.

In work environments, non-wage benefits like healthcare and retirement matter. Flexible schedules and workplace safety, though not directly valued monetarily, are important to workers. Studies show people might sacrifice 20% of wages to avoid frequent schedule changes, with 80% of job satisfaction or dissatisfaction linked to non-wage reasons.

Strong evidence indicates unions improve fringe benefits and non-wage aspects, enhancing workers' wellbeing. Comparisons show union workers are more likely to get certain amenities. Robust studies confirm unions significantly improve work environments, benefiting workers and families.

Modern union demographics show equal representation among men and women, with Black men having a 13% union representation rate in 2021. Unions promote equality within firms through anti-discrimination measures and fair wage-setting practices, reducing race and gender gaps. Studies confirm unions have closed wage gaps among different groups.

Unions' positive effects extend to nonunion workers. Firms competing with unions may raise wages or improve work environments. Positive spillovers exist, with a 1% increase in private-sector union membership translating to a 0.3% increase in nonunion wages, especially for workers without a college degree.

Unions also benefit communities, enhancing social capital and civic engagement. Union members vote more, and those in union households contribute more to community activities, charity, and volunteer work.

Important Takeaway

Communities come in different shapes and sizes, for various goals and purposes. But one thing you'll notice with all of them is that they are there to serve their members. You can't have a Chinese community that is serving non-Chinese people, just as you can't have a professional association that is fighting for non-members. The White South Africans created the apartheid system to ensure resources and the best land and opportunities went to the white community in South Africa.

The Patel & Rothschild families have built vast amounts of wealth, power and influence for their family members. And while The United Arab Emirates is one of the wealthiest nations in the world and has a generous social system that gives citizens free education, free health-care, even free land and housing, it's a luxury that's only given to Emiratis, not the immigrants. If you want to build a thriving community, make sure you define who is part of your community and make sure you give all the benefits, opportunities and preferential treatment to your community members ONLY.

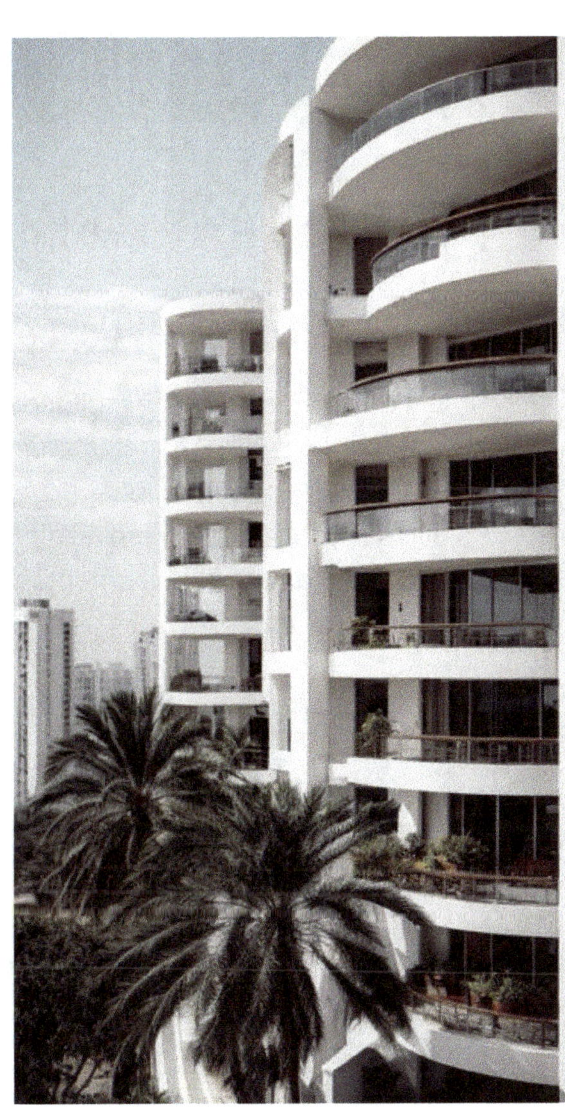

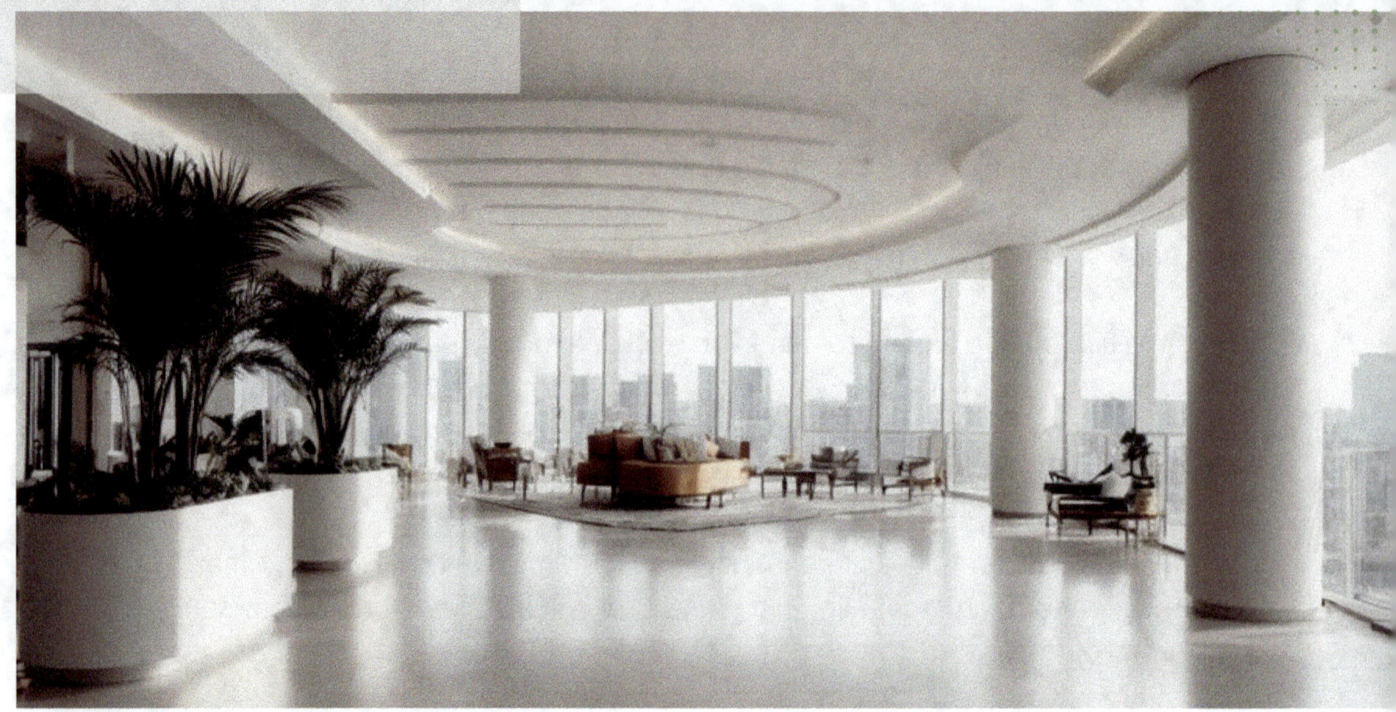

CHAPTER FOUR

IT TAKES A VILLAGE TO RAISE A CHILD

The Crucial Role of Community in Child Development

Child development is a multifaceted process influenced by various factors, and the role of community is paramount in shaping a child's growth, well-being, and overall development. From social and emotional aspects to cognitive and physical dimensions, the community plays a crucial role in providing the necessary environment for a child to thrive. Let's explore why raising a child in a community is vital if you want them to turn out a well-adjusted human being.

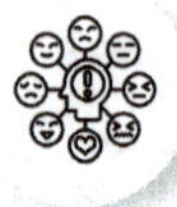

1. Social and Emotional Development:

Communities serve as the first social environment for children outside their immediate family. Interactions with peers, neighbors, and community members contribute significantly to the development of social skills, emotional intelligence, and the ability to navigate relationships. Positive social experiences within a community setting foster empathy, cooperation, and a sense of belonging.

2. Cultural and Identity Formation:

Communities are rich with cultural diversity, exposing children to various traditions, languages, and customs. This exposure aids in the formation of a child's cultural identity and helps them appreciate and understand different perspectives. Community involvement provides a sense of heritage and belonging, contributing to a child's self-esteem and a positive sense of identity.

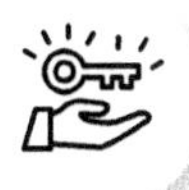

3. Educational Opportunities:

Communities play a crucial role in providing educational opportunities for children. Local schools, libraries, and community centers serve as essential hubs for learning and skill development. Access to quality education within the community ensures that children have the foundational knowledge and skills necessary for cognitive development.

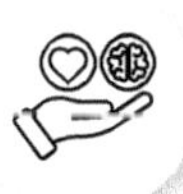

4. Physical Well-being:

The physical environment within a community directly impacts a child's well-being. Access to parks, recreational spaces, and healthcare facilities contributes to physical development and overall health. Communities that prioritize safety and provide opportunities for physical activity foster healthy habits, reducing the risk of childhood obesity and related health issues.

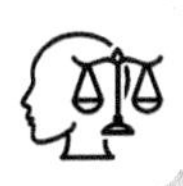

5. Moral and Ethical Values:

Communities often play a role in instilling moral and ethical values in children. Through religious institutions, community organizations, and shared cultural values, children learn about principles such as honesty, respect, and responsibility. These values form the foundation for ethical decision-making and character development.

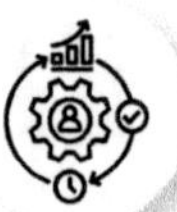

6. Support Systems:

A strong community serves as a support system for families, offering resources and assistance that positively impact child development. Networks of neighbors, friends, and community organizations can provide emotional support, child-care assistance, and access to essential services. These support systems contribute to a child's sense of security and stability.

Different Roles Within the Community

Communities are made up of different people doing different jobs that help the community. These roles work together to make sure everyone's needs are taken care of, and the community does well. Let's look at some important roles people have in a community.

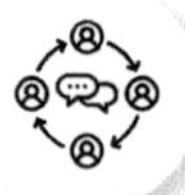

1. Community Leaders:

Leaders play a pivotal role in guiding and shaping the direction of a community. This includes elected officials, local government representatives, and community organizers. They make decisions, implement policies, and advocate for the interests of the community. Effective leaders foster collaboration, address challenges, and work towards the betterment of the community.

2. Educators and Mentors:

Teachers, tutors, and mentors contribute significantly to community development by providing education and guidance to individuals of all ages. Their roles extend beyond traditional classrooms, encompassing community centers, after-school programs, and mentorship initiatives. Education and mentorship empower individuals, fostering personal growth and contributing to a community's intellectual capital.

3. Social Workers and Advocates:

Social workers and advocates work towards addressing social issues within the community. They support vulnerable populations, advocate for social justice, and work on initiatives that address poverty, inequality, and discrimination. Their roles contribute to creating a more equitable and inclusive community.

4. Community Builders and Organizers:

Individuals who actively engage in community building and organizing play a crucial role in fostering a sense of cohesion and connection. They organize events, facilitate community projects, and create spaces for individuals to come together. Community builders strengthen social bonds and contribute to a positive community identity.

5. Business Owners and Entrepreneurs:

Business owners and entrepreneurs contribute to the economic vitality of the community. Through local businesses, they create job opportunities, stimulate economic growth, and contribute to the unique character of the community. Supporting local businesses is often seen as a way to strengthen the community's economic foundation.

6. Caretakers and Parents:

Parents and caretakers play fundamental roles in the well-being of families and, by extension, the community. Their responsibilities include nurturing and raising the next generation, creating a supportive home environment, and actively participating in community activities. The values instilled by parents contribute to the overall culture of the community.

7. Technology and Innovation Leaders:

In an increasingly interconnected world, individuals involved in technology and innovation contribute to a community's growth. They may develop digital infrastructure, support local tech initiatives, or provide educational resources, contributing to the community's adaptability in the face of technological advancements.

The Consequences of Forgetting the Need for Community

In a fast-paced and individualistic world, the importance of community is sometimes overlooked or underestimated. When individuals forget or neglect the need for community, various consequences can impact both personal well-being and the societal fabric. Let's explore these consequences in-depth.

1. Social Isolation and Loneliness:

Forgetting the need for community often leads to increased social isolation and loneliness. Humans are inherently social beings, and a lack of meaningful connections can result in feelings of isolation, which, over time, can have detrimental effects on mental health. Loneliness is associated with increased stress, depression, and a decline in overall well-being.

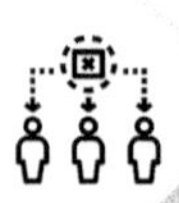

2. Lack of Emotional Support:

Communities serve as a source of emotional support during challenging times. Forgetting the need for community means missing out on a network of individuals who can provide comfort, empathy, and understanding. Without this emotional support system, individuals may find it more difficult to cope with life's ups and downs.

4. Diminished Sense of Belonging:

A strong sense of belonging is a fundamental human need. Communities provide a sense of identity and belongingness that contributes to an individual's overall well-being. Forgetting the importance of community diminishes this sense of belonging, leaving individuals feeling disconnected and detached from the broader social fabric.

5. Loss of Collective Benefits:

Communities provide collective benefits such as shared resources, safety, and collaborative problem-solving. Forgetting the need for community means missing out on these collective advantages, hindering the potential for communal progress and shared prosperity.

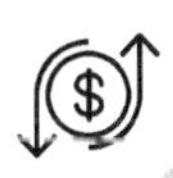

6. Loss of Financial growth:

Not having a community means you miss out on making more money. Having a community behind you means you can ask your community for work if you're unemployed or want to change career, or you can ask your community for help to fund your next million dollar business ideas.

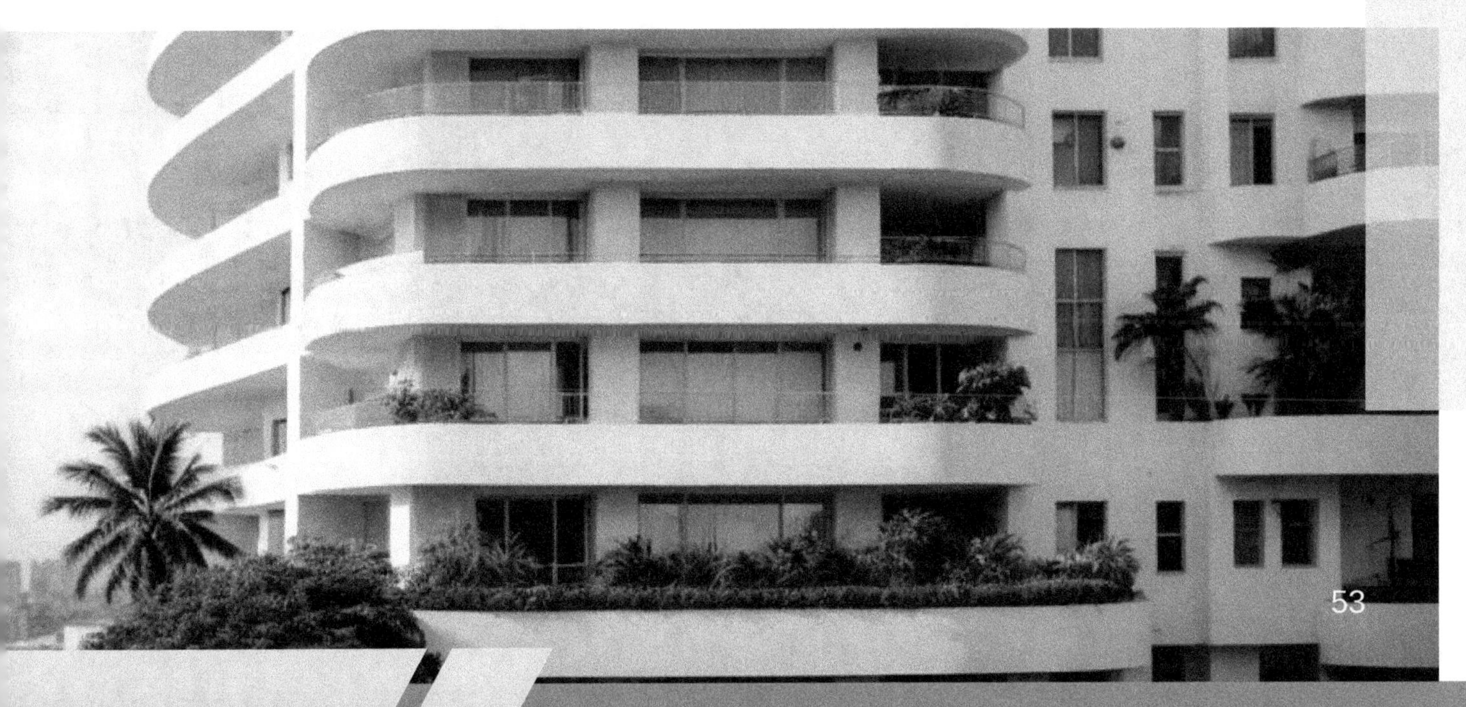

CHAPTER FIVE

THE VISION OF THE MODERN AFRICAN COMMUNITY

Purpose and Mission

The purpose of The Modern African Community is profoundly simple yet incredibly powerful: to rebuild prosperous African communities. We're on a mission to rewrite the narrative of homeownership, creating a future where it's not just an aspiration but an achievable reality for all on-code Africans across the globe.

We believe in the strength of unity and shared goals. Our mission is to build functional, scalable, and thriving wealthy African communities across the globe just like the Chinese, the Whites & the Jews have done. By investing in this mission, you're not just buying a property; you're becoming part of a movement that's going to change the world.

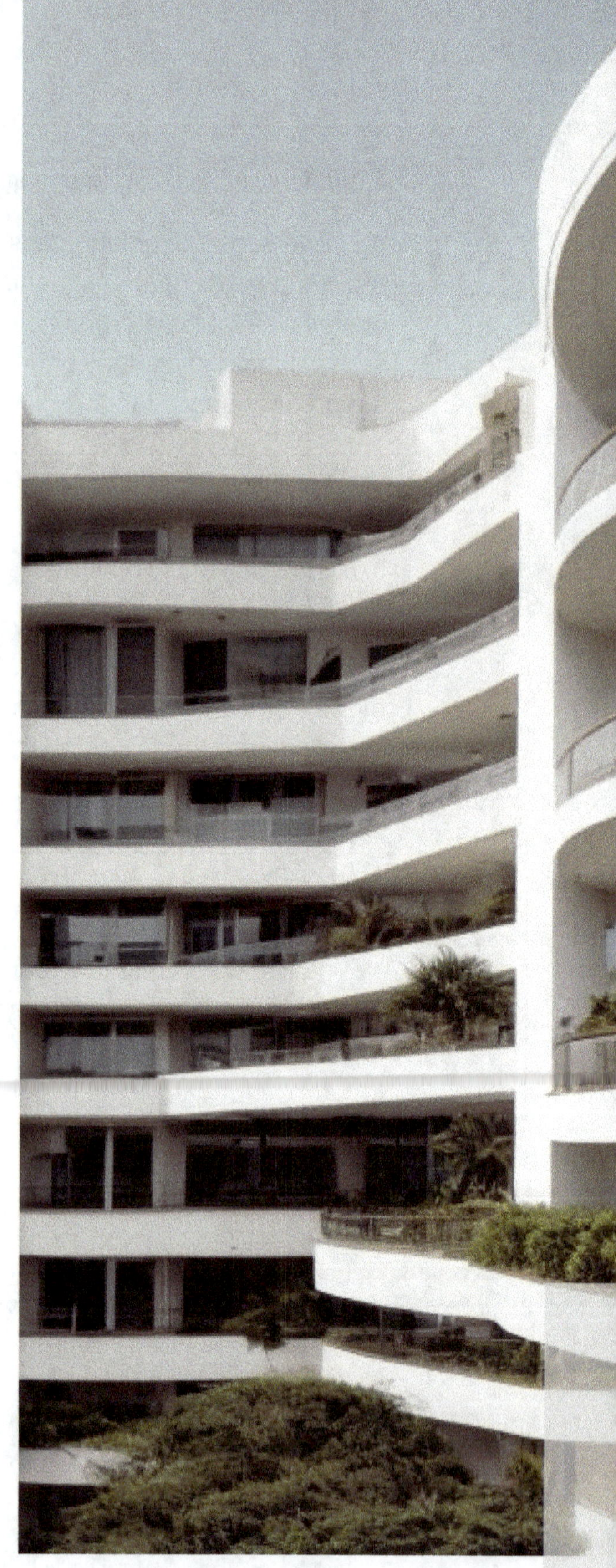

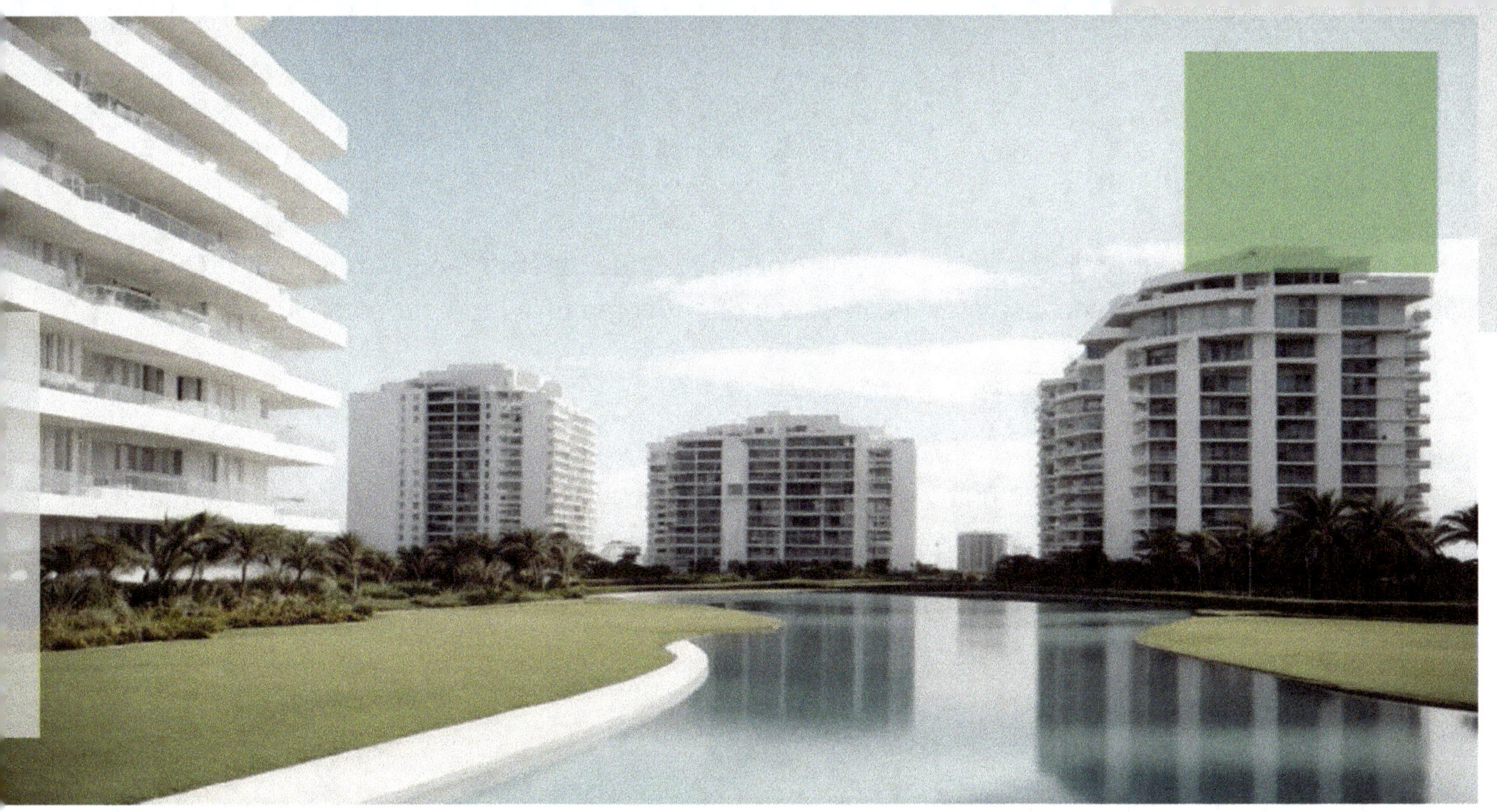

Core Values & Code of Conduct

Our core values & code of conduct aren't just words on paper; they're the guiding principles that steer our ship towards prosperity. As you become a member of The Modern African Community, you'll find that these values permeate every aspect of our community.

Ubuntu - I am because we are: This African philosophy reminds us that our individual success is directly tied to the success of our community. When one prospers, we all prosper. It's about fostering a sense of togetherness, support, and shared achievements.

Putting the Group Before the Individual: In our community, we prioritize the well-being of all members. It's about valuing collective success over individual gain. When we act for the greater good, everyone benefits, including you as an individual.

Group Economics: By pooling our resources and working together, we unlock financial opportunities that might be out of reach individually. It's about strengthening our collective financial power and creating opportunities for wealth-building.

Ubuntu Philosophy

Ubuntu is more than just a word; it's a way of life at The Modern African Community. This African philosophy encapsulates the essence of our community and our commitment to one another.

I Am Because We Are: Ubuntu reminds us that our individual well-being is intricately tied to the well-being of our community. It's about lifting each other up, supporting one another, and celebrating collective success.

Community Over Individual: In our community, we put the group before the individual. We prioritize shared prosperity, respect, and inclusivity. Ubuntu isn't just a concept; it's a living philosophy that guides our interactions and behaviors.

By embracing Ubuntu, we create a community where every member is valued, and every voice is heard.

As you dive deeper into the The Modern African Community, you'll discover that it's not just about owning a home; it's about becoming part of a transformative movement where prosperity, support, and unity reign supreme. Thrive, and sustainability is a way of life. We put the group first, practice group economics and hold each other accountable through a single value system - a strong code of conduct.

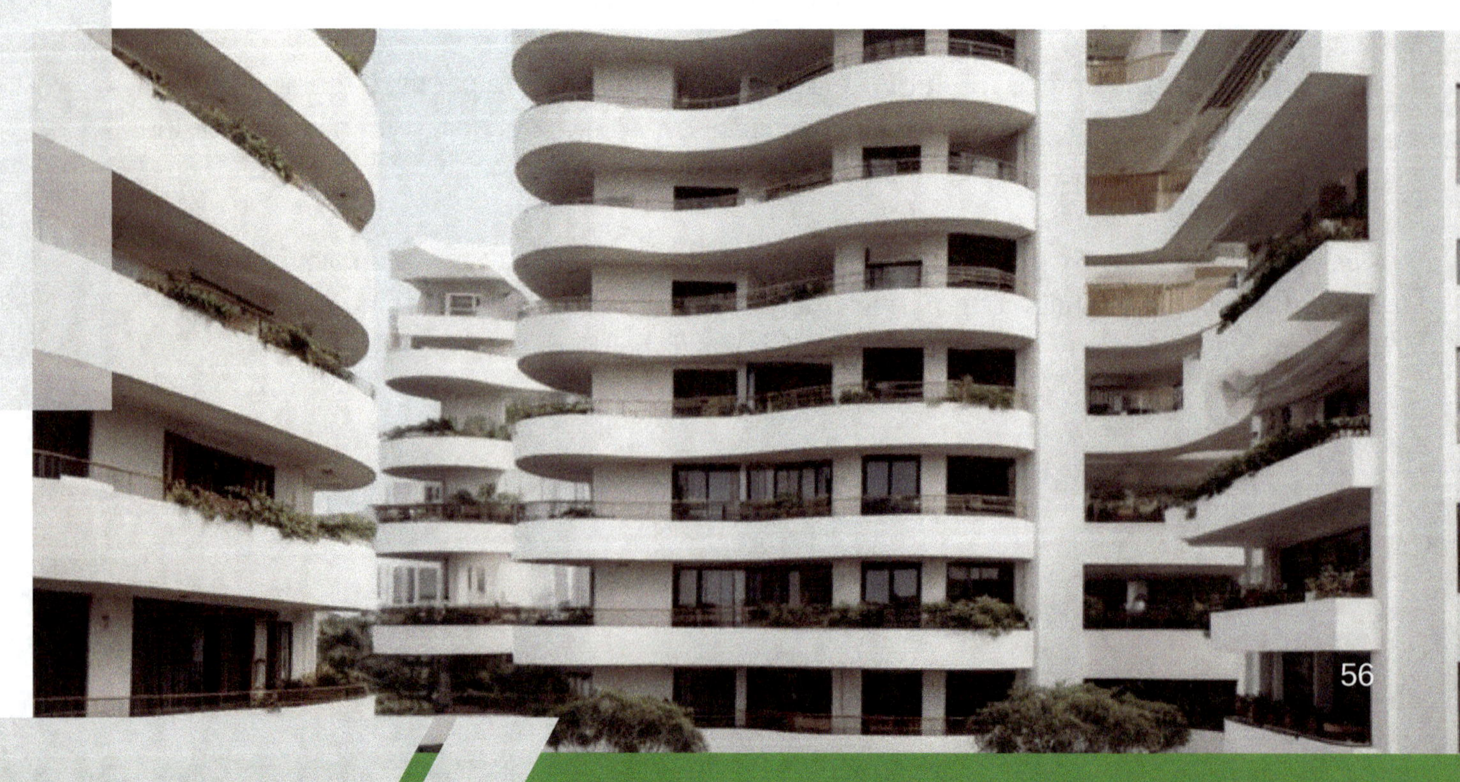

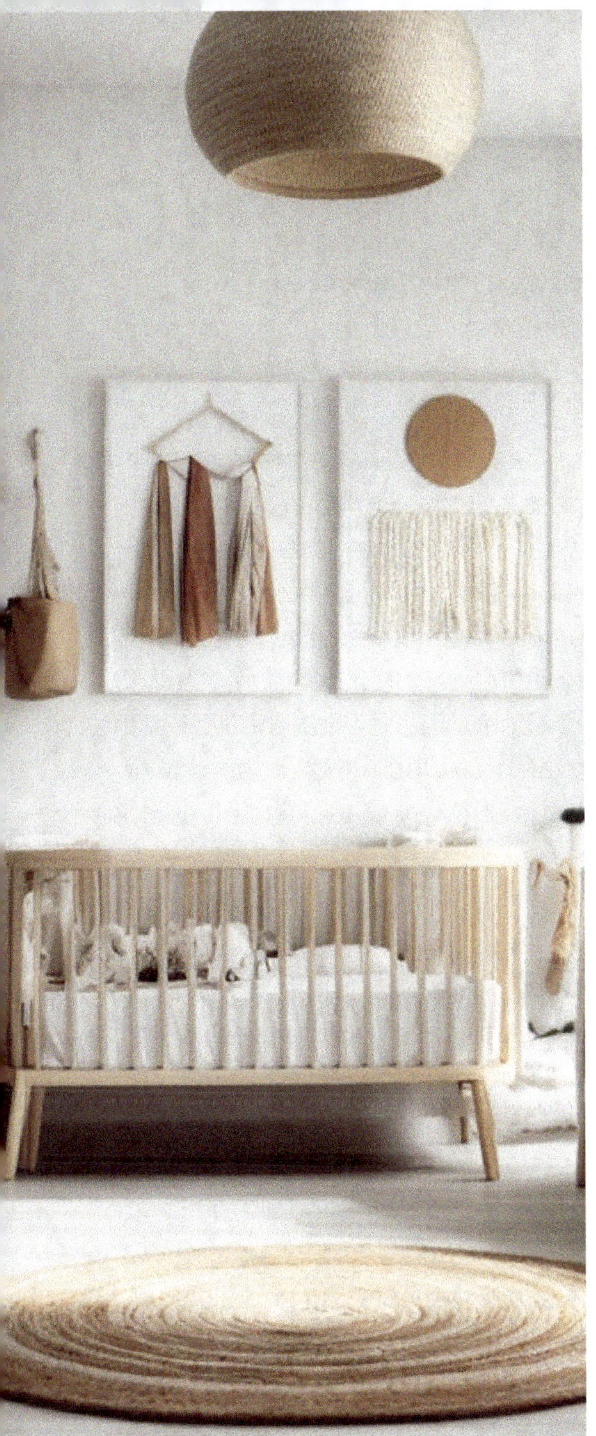

CHAPTER SIX

THE MODERN AFRICAN COMMUNITY

WHAT SETS US APART

At The Modern African Community, we're not just offering beautiful homes to live in. We are building a community where we put the collective group's interest above everything else. We believe that having a community where everyone is on-code with each other and practices group economics with each other will allow us to build a community that is powerful and wealthy.

We want to build a community where we are all well-off business owners, not just 10% of us. We believe in UBUNTU and that if we look out for the collective, the collective will look out for us. By focusing on helping the group, we are indirectly also helping ourselves. We want to create a system that can be replicated across the continent of Africa and the rest of the globe.

We want to change the world, make it affordable and rewarding to be part of the EXCLUSIVE, POWERFUL & WEALTHY **Modern African Community.**

CO-OP Ownership

At The Modern African Community, we're rewriting the rules of homeownership by introducing the CO-OP ownership model. This model will eventually allow us to sell homes worth $300,000 for just $30,000. Here's how it works and why it matters:

Collective Ownership: Our residents collectively own and manage at least 80% of the businesses in the community. This means that profits generated by these businesses flow back into the community, benefiting everyone. It's a model that fosters economic empowerment and shared success. We will allow our members to start their own small ventures and as long as the ventures aren't selling to the community and are generating less than $100k in turn-over then they are free to own it outright 100%.

However, if a member or members create a business that is directly selling to the community and turning over more than $100k annually, then the business will have to be sold to a community collective for 3 times its annual profits by max year 5 of being operational. This rule is in place in order to keep businesses that are scalable in the hands of the collective. We don't want to end up in a community where 10% of the community are really wealthy because they're just excellent business people, while everyone else is just getting by as employees & consumers. That's not what our community is about. This is what the rest of the world and most nations are about. But as we can see from taking a closer look at society, it only leads to crime, poverty, resentment and inequality. This is our way of tackling all of those symptoms.

Exclusive Opportunities: For the budding entrepreneurs among us, The Modern African Community opens the door to a world of opportunities. Whether it's a local shop, a restaurant, or another venture, you have the very exclusive right to open businesses in our communities and profit from an upper middle class demographic. Imagine there are 100 stores in our community, if you're an accountant - you'll have the RIGHT to offer your accountancy services to the 100 businesses, and as long as you're qualified and providing a good quality service, the 100 businesses will be obligated by our Code of Conduct to hire you, before they ever hire an outside accountant. Now imagine all the opportunities that will be there for us; clothing brands, furniture stores, wholesale suppliers, catering services; whatever product or services you wish to offer to us, will be made available to you as a community member, whereas outsider competition will be required to jump through red-tape and hurdles that won't exist for you! As a community that owns the land and premises we have the power and right to make these rules & bylaws. Have you ever seen a bunch of African owned stores in a Chinese community like China-Town X? Nope? It's because they have a similar code. They lock-out the non-members and offer exclusive opportunities to their members only.

$500 Monthly Payments

Here's where it gets even more exciting. Instead of you paying rent or a mortgage, The Modern African Community pays you! As a resident, your household will receive $500 every month. We'll be able to do this because the businesses in the community will be owned by us and because we will practice group economics with each other. Imagine what that extra income could mean for your life.

If you took out a mortgage or loan, it would help finance the purchase of your home. If you're interested in starting an online side-hustle, you'd be able to do that. If you need a little extra cash to help out elderly parents or send your child to an international school, that $500 per month would be able to help you with that. What other community or real estate development is thinking about you to this length?

What other development company wants to set you and your family up for generational wealth the way The Modern African Community does?

Location and Development Details

Now, let's talk about the place you'll soon call home. The (first) Modern African Community is going to be strategically located along Kenya's Coastline, just a stone's throw away from the vibrant heart of Mombasa. Here's what you can expect from our development:

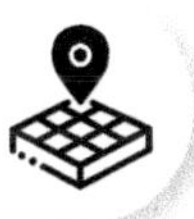

Prime Location: Our development is planned to be situated in a prime location in Kilifi, known for its serene surroundings, pristine beaches along the East African Ocean and easy accessibility to Milindi, Vipingo & Mombasa. We're also looking into building near Likoni, Mombasa -but ultimately, we will decide where to buy land and develop the community collectively as a group.

Development Plans: Our development is a carefully planned masterpiece. We're creating a thriving community with a mix of residential and business spaces, all designed to promote a sense of belonging and prosperity.

Amenities: From parks and communal spaces to modern facilities, schools and business outlets; The Modern African Community is designed to offer a holistic living experience. We're not just building homes; we're creating a community where everything you need is within reach.

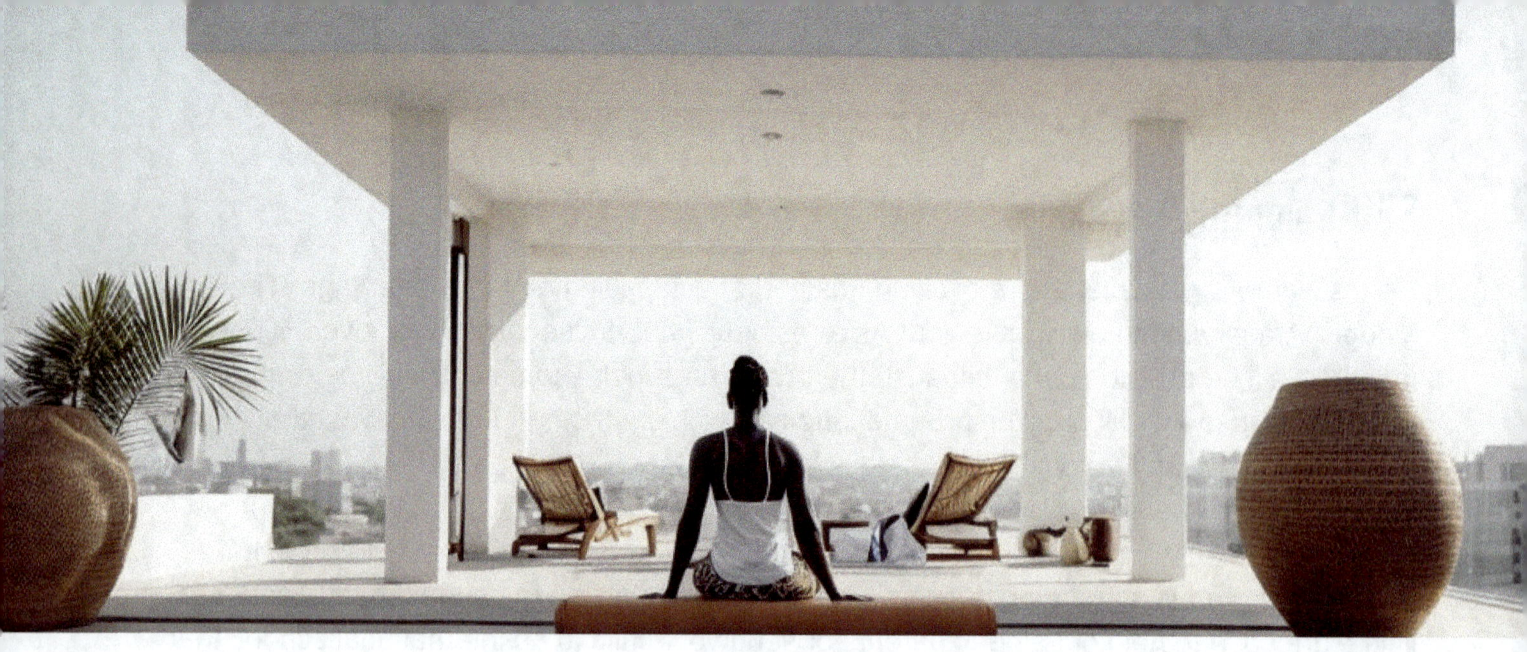

The 15-Minute Walkable City

Picture this: You step out of your home, and within a 15-minute walk, you're at your workplace, a local restaurant, or a beautiful green park. That's the concept of a 15-Minute Walkable City that The Modern African Community embraces.

Convenience: Say goodbye to long commutes and hours spent in traffic. In our walkable city, everything you need is conveniently close by, reducing stress and giving you more precious time in your day.

Sustainability and Groon Living

Our commitment to sustainability goes beyond just words. We're building green living spaces that promote eco-friendly practices.

Green Communal Spaces: Imagine having access to lush green spaces right within your community. It's a place to connect with nature, unwind, and recharge.

Minimalism: We believe in quality over quantity. Minimalistic living promotes a clutter-free environment, both in your home and in your life.

As you can see, the The Modern African Community experience is more than just buying a property; it's about becoming part of a thriving, close-knit community where homeownership is affordable and businesses are owned by the collective community.

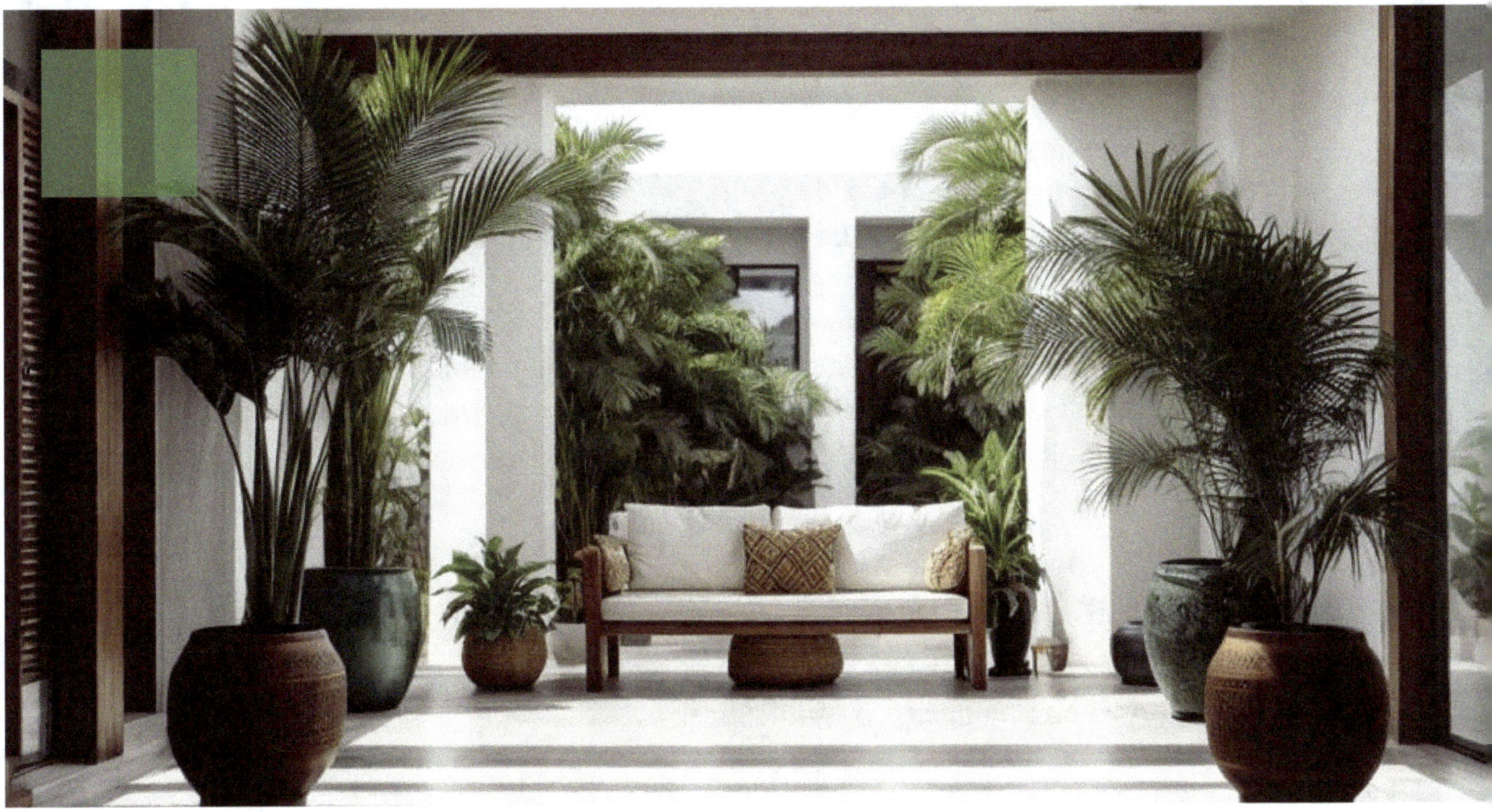

CHAPTER SEVEN

WHAT TO EXPECT FROM THE MODERN AFRICAN COMMUNITY

Preparing for Your Move

Before you make the move to your new The Modern African Community home, there are a few essential steps to consider:

Financial Planning: Take some time to review your finances and ensure that you're financially prepared for the move. Have your savings and credit score in order if you plan on getting a loan or mortgage for the purchase.

Customization: If you've chosen off-plan purchasing, you'll have the opportunity to customize your new home to your liking. Consider your design preferences and start planning how you'd like to personalize your space. Please note that customization could drastically increase the price of an apartment unit.

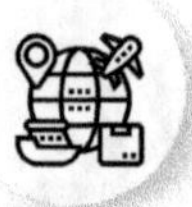 **Logistics:** Moving involves logistics, so plan ahead. Whether you're relocating from another city or just down the street, having a clear plan can make the process smoother. Let us know how we can help you with this.

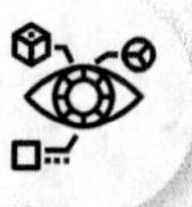 **Embrace the Community Vision:** As you prepare to become a member of The Modern African Community, it's important to embrace our vision and values. This is a journey towards collective prosperity, so keep that in mind as you make your preparations.

Welcoming New Members

At The Modern African Community, we take pride in our welcoming and inclusive environment. As a new member, you can expect:

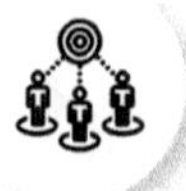 **Orientation:** We provide an orientation process to help you settle in seamlessly. You'll receive information about the community, your benefits, and how to get involved in different community events & activities.

 **Support:** Our community is here to support you. If you have questions or need assistance, don't hesitate to reach out to fellow members or our dedicated team.

 **Inclusivity:** We believe that every member's voice matters. You'll be encouraged to participate in discussions, meetings, and decision-making processes that impact the community.

Community Events and Opportunities

The Modern African Community is not just a place to live; it's a place to thrive. Here's a taste of what awaits you:

 **Community Events:** We'll host a variety of community events, from cultural celebrations to educational workshops. These events are an excellent way to connect with your neighbors and build relationships.

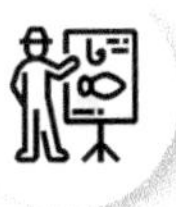

Workshops and Training: As a Modern African Community member, you'll have access to workshops and training sessions that can enhance your skills and knowledge. Whether it's financial literacy, entrepreneurship, or personal development, we're here to support your growth.

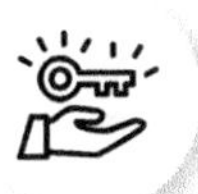

Business Opportunities: Remember, you're not just a homeowner; you're also part of a CO-OP ownership model. This means you have the opportunity to invest in and run businesses within the community. Keep an eye out for business opportunities that align with your interests and goals.

Building Relationships

Building connections with fellow community members is a key part of the The Modern African Community experience:

Engage: Attend community events and engage in discussions. Share your ideas, experiences, and talents with others. The more you engage, the richer your community experience will be.

Support Each Other: In our community, we lift each other up. Whether it's helping a neighbor, sharing resources, or collaborating on projects, supporting one another is at the core of our values.

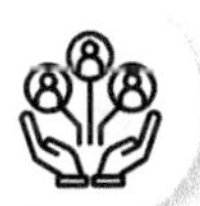

Join Committees: Consider joining committees or groups within the community that align with your interests or expertise. This is a fantastic way to contribute and build relationships with like-minded members.

As you embark on your journey with The Modern African Community, remember that you're not just joining a housing development; you're becoming part of a thriving, supportive, and inclusive community. Your journey will be shaped by the relationships you build and the experiences you create together.

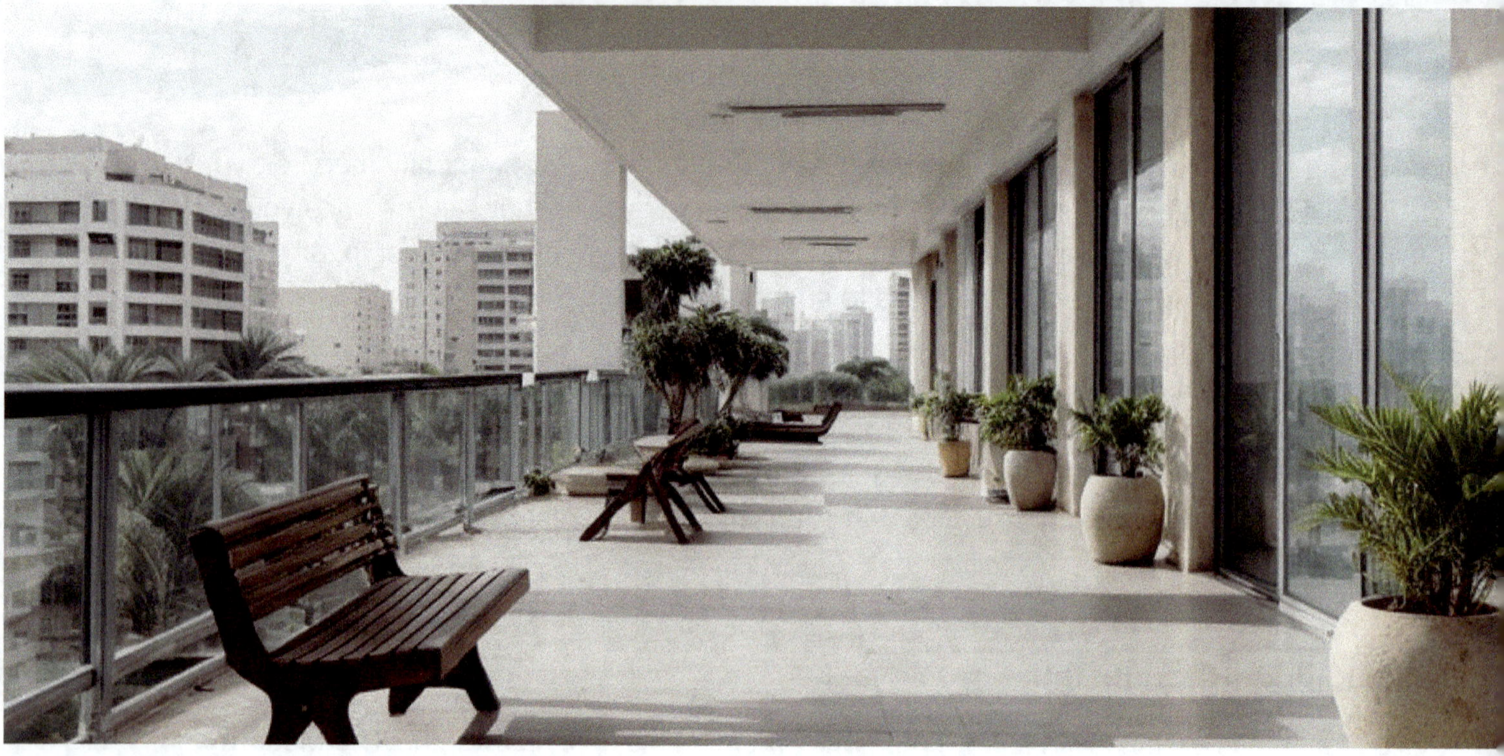

CHAPTER EIGHT

SECURING YOUR SPOT & FAQ

We believe that taking action today can lead to a brighter tomorrow. Here's why you should act now:

 **Limited Availability:** We have a total of 200 spots available, and we expect they'll be bought up quickly. There's huge demand and excitement surrounding The Modern African Community. Don't miss out on this incredible opportunity to become a member if our values align with each other.

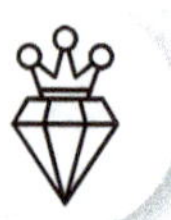 **Exclusive Benefits:** As a member, you'll have access to exclusive benefits, including $500 monthly payouts, CO-OP ownership opportunities, exclusive business & job opportunities and a supportive community. The sooner you join, the sooner you can start enjoying these benefits.

 **Changing Lives:** By securing your spot, you're not just investing in a property; you're investing in a vision that's going to change lives and rebuild prosperous African communities. Every member plays a crucial role in making this vision a reality.

How to Join

Joining The Modern African Community is a straightforward process.

1. **Complete Survey:** Complete a short survey that lets us learn more about you and your values. If we feel like you'd be a good community member, we'll send you an invite to join our private whatsapp group.

2. **Join WhatsApp Group:** Join our private Whatsapp group for updates, news & access to special offers.

3. **Secure Your Spot:** We'll host weekly webinars and allow a limited number of people to get early access to the development & community.

FAQ

We have beautifully crafted out answers to some common questions and concerns potential members may have:

Q: Can I visit the development site before making a decision?

A: Once all 200 units are sold out and we've collectively decided on where we're going to buy land and build our community then we would absolutely encourage you and your family to visit our site and get a feel for the location.

Q: What if I change my mind after making the deposit?

A: We understand that circumstances can change. If you decide not to proceed, your deposit will be refunded as per our terms & conditions and someone else will take your spot.

Q: Can I sell my property in the future?

A: You will be able to sell the property in the future, but please note that you'll have to sell it back to us (the community) for the same amount that you bought it for. This is NOT a project where we want speculators and investors out for a quick profit. We want people that want to be part of a community and have access to affordable living thanks to our unique business model where the businesses in the community are owned by the collective group allowing each household to get paid $500 each month in passive income.

Q: Do you accept partners?

A: We are looking for strategic partners to help us sell these units, local governments willing to host us & work with us to make this project a reality in their county, and other people that would be able to add value to the project.

Q: What is the timeline for the development's completion?

A: We're committed to delivering a high-quality development that aligns with our vision and values. We expect the project to take 2-3 years to be fully completed. But you know what they say, good things take their time.

As you consider securing your spot within The Modern African Community, remember that you're not just investing in a home; you're investing in a community that's redefining the future of homeownership.

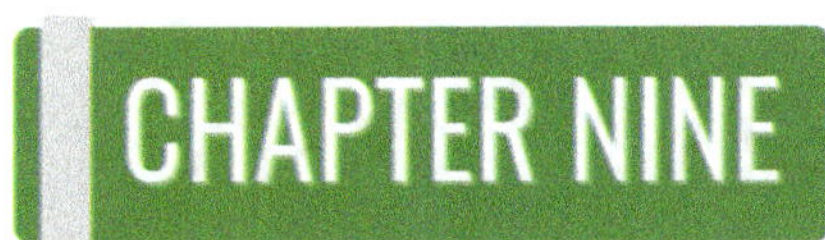

CHAPTER NINE

CONCLUSION

Thank You

I'd like to thank you for having spent your time reading this book, it means a lot to us. Hope you have learned a few things about the importance of having a community behind you, and I hope it has motivated you to want to join the FIRST Modern African Community that's going to help us build wealth and prosper as a collective.

Recap of the Benefits of Join Modern African Community

The Modern African Community isn't just a housing development; it's a new way of making homes affordable, it's a vision for thriving African communities across the globe and it's a dream & hope of millions of Africans that want to see a better world for African people across the globe. Here are the key benefits you'll enjoy as a member:

Affordable Homeownership: Secure a home for yourself and your family without the burdensome costs of traditional mortgages. Buy off-plan and save big.

$500 Monthly Payouts: Receive $500 every month, rewarding you for being part of our community. Use the money to subsidize your mortgage or just use it to improve your lifestyle. It's up to you. Just remember to practice group economics.

CO-OP Ownership: Join a community where residents collectively own and manage businesses, ensuring prosperity for all.

Sustainable Living: Embrace a green and sustainable lifestyle in our walkable city, surrounded by green communal spaces.

Exclusive Opportunities: Get access to EXCLUSIVE business & job opportunities. You'll have first right of refusal to work & business deals. Once we're fully established, we'll even offer free basic health care, free basic schooling, free child care services & other exclusive perks to our members.

Ubuntu Philosophy: Be part of a community that values Ubuntu, where unity, support, and collective well-being are central.

JOIN US & LET'S BUILD THE MODERN AFRICAN COMMUNITY

The time for action is now. Don't miss out on this once in a life-time opportunity to be part of the first Modern African community that's going to change the rules of homeownership and wealth building.

HOW TO JOIN

Join The Modern African Community in just a few simple steps.

1. **Complete Survey: Complete a short survey that lets us learn more about you and your values.** If we feel like you'd be a good community member, we'll send you an invite to join our private whatsapp group. Visit **https://african.community/step1** to complete the survey.

2. **Join WhatsApp Group:** Join our private Whatsapp group for updates, news & access to special offers.

3. **Secure Your Spot:** We'll host weekly webinars and allow a limited number of people to get early access to the development & community.

THANK YOU AND REMEMBER, STAY ON CODE, PRACTICE GROUP ECONOMICS AND PUT THE COMMUNITY FIRST. THE REST WILL SORT ITSELF OUT.